D0006226

Enjoy Teaching

Helpful Hints for the Classroom

Carol Gildner

The Scarecrow Press, Inc.
A Scarecrow Education Book
Lanham, Maryland, and London
2001

SCARECROW PRESS, INC.
A Scarecrow Education Book

Published in the United States of America
by Scarecrow Press, Inc.
4720 Boston Way, Lanham, Maryland 20706
www.scarecroweducation.com

4 Pleydell Gardens, Folkestone
Kent CT20 2DN, England

British Library Cataloguing in Publication Information Available

Library of Congress Cataloging-in-Publication Data

Gildner, Carol.
    Enjoy teaching : helpful hints for the classroom / Carol Gildner.
        p. cm. — (A Scarecrow education book)
    Includes bibliographical references and index.
    ISBN 0-8108-4050-2 (alk. paper) — ISBN 0-8108-4051-0 (pbk. : alk. paper)
        1. Teaching—Handbooks, manuals, etc. 2. Classroom management—Handbooks,
    manuals, etc. 3. Teachers—Handbooks, manuals, etc. I. Title. II. Series.
    LB1025.3 .G445 2001
        371.102—dc21   2001020694

♾™ The paper used in this publication meets the minimum requirements of
American National Standard for Information Sciences—Permanence of
Paper for Printed Library Materials, ANSI/NISO Z39.48-1992.
Manufactured in the United States of America.

To John Gildner,
who inspired and encouraged me
and edited much of this book

Contents

ഇൻയ

Acknowledgments

ℰᏅℂᏅ

This book would not be possible without the assistance of many people. First are the children, who are truly the main teachers of teachers. One learns from students every day, and life is enriched by time spent with them. In addition, so many of my coworkers and my own professional teachers have shaped my ideas about teaching. Their examples have made significant contributions to concepts expressed in this book.

I want particularly to thank the following individuals: Carolyn Cardle, Mary Ann DiSerafino, Rick DiSerafino, Cynthia Ditmars, Bettie J. Kimmel, Nikki Lanzaron, Bonnie Macdonald, Cameron Millspaugh, Stacy Millspaugh, Kathleen Snore, and Nancy Wigant.

Introduction

ℰᏋᏝᏒ

Teachers are almost too busy to read another book. However, they are also excited to learn ideas that will help them teach successfully. New teachers hope for help that is easy to find; experienced instructors look for needed answers that can be found quickly. The goal of this book is to present short essays of topics of high interest or importance in education. Experienced teachers often agree on these points and would like to share them with anyone who needs to know the information. The reader is invited to begin at any point and pick and choose topics that seem important at that time.

Many education books provide catchy paragraphs and sets of rules to help teachers. They don't really say enough to tell a teacher how to apply the ideas. An aim of this book is to briefly explain the how and why of a concept. Often, there are specific lessons or a graph or other supporting materials for clearer understanding and immediate use. The book attempts to state, and sometimes clarify, principles of *successful* teaching. In as many situations as possible, it suggests practical lessons or techniques a teacher may copy or adapt to his or her own classroom.

Thirty years of pleasant classroom experience inspired me to write this book. Many of these suggestions and ideas were shared with a series of student teachers. The student teachers reported that the ideas were most helpful when they too were regular classroom teachers. These new teachers said it was invaluable to be able, for example, to think of ten remedies for a problem.

Change is constant in teaching. One needs to respond to new students and new realities of society. Fresh ideas energize teachers. Hopefully this book will aid beginning teachers as well as teachers seeking to polish their teaching skills. It seems important, in these days of heavy rhetoric about problems in schools, to tell a positive story. Many teachers consider the job exciting, meaningful, and enjoyable. This book is an attempt to clarify this positive attitude to help create a successful atmosphere in the classroom.

Chapter 1

ℰℭ

Beginning School

In the Beginning

Teachers are lucky people. They have the satisfaction of beginning and ending their school year. Other workers in business complain that days simply follow days of similar tasks, with no end in sight before retirement.

It's exciting and a bit scary to begin a new school year or semester or quarter. The tension involved can make one sharper, if preparations have been made. A minimum of four days before children arrive in the classroom is usually needed. Of course, many teachers use more time than this, but some preparation is essential.

Class lists are needed as soon as possible to plan for specific students. Focusing on these children lays the groundwork for decision making that is child-centered. Plans are different for groups of thirty-seven than for classes of nineteen. Sometimes information about the children is available from administration, the special education department, guidance, or a health aide.

Days before the school session begins, a teacher can walk into the assigned classroom and visualize how it will work best for the

1

goals he or she has. It may be wise to use some graph paper and draw up possible floor plans of the classroom. Where would the teacher's desk be most convenient? Many teachers like to face the door to stay aware of doorway and hallway movements. Some teachers arrange files and bookcases behind their desks to aid in convenient organized storage of materials. Certain teachers put tables at sides of their desks to make handouts and returned materials easily available to the children. Some teachers like to use these tables as a convenient place to locate a computer and printer. Other teachers don't want those tables there at all, making a sort of wall between the children and themselves; they want to be more readily accessible to the children.

Arrangement of student seating controls much of the direction of teaching style. A teacher who wants to encourage cooperative learning groups four desks to face each other or seats children at tables. A teacher who wants to strengthen discipline and classroom quiet arranges the desks in straight rows, with some distance between. There are many other seating combinations: in circles, pairs, etc. There are reasons why any of these seating arrangements may be chosen. Teachers may also change the student seating from time to time to follow certain lesson strategies.

Location of materials in closets, shelves, and other storage areas is also important to the smooth functioning of the classroom. It can be helpful to have many available flat spaces and tables for student projects, displays, locations for specific activities, or seating a child to encourage behavior improvement.

Visualizing the setup of the classroom helps when establishing lesson goals and plans for a school year or semester. The setting will influence the students' learning accomplishments. Knowing the numbers and names of students and the classroom setup can make planning curriculum goals and lessons more realistic before school begins.

Studying the curriculum guide from the school system and using a planning calendar are helpful to set benchmarks for hoped-for units of teaching in time blocks. A teacher needs to try to fit the curriculum into the time allowed, shortening some units if necessary. It may be wise to allow a catch-up day between each unit to allow for school emergencies and for slower progress by some classes. An instructor needs to be able to adapt planned lessons to fit the calendar, too. Without broad plans, class progress may simply stay with original units too long to reach the curriculum's promised goals and accomplish benchmarks.

Certain classes will find the curriculum goals too difficult. Some teachers modify the lessons for these slower groups. Many simply cover less material. The subject controls this to some extent. Math and languages are examples of subjects whose progress is driven by student ability. However, exceptional teachers will use techniques to stimulate learning and challenge students and will accomplish the complete syllabus. Other classes will move even more quickly than the teacher anticipated and will need to have more enrichment and depth or projects added to their teaching plan.

Setting up a classroom floor plan chart, moving the furniture, filling in teaching benchmark steps on a calendar to establish a basic plan to cover the curriculum, organizing class lists and school directives, and preparing a grade book and blank seating chart are essential for a smooth beginning of school. Once this structure is established, remaining time can be given to decorating the classroom and beginning some professional relationships with fellow teachers. It is wise to visit the library, guidance department, health suite, office, etc., and meet staff personnel. Seek out the custodians, cafeteria staff, security people, and bus drivers as well. Everyone works together as a team in a well-run school, and knowing the people on this team will aid this cohesiveness and help any teacher enjoy the school and gain the sense that each person plays an important part in success of the children.

Lesson Planning

Lesson plans vary by class subject, age of students, needs of students, skill level of the teacher, size of space allowed, equipment and supplies available, and endless other factors. Teaching is something like a card game, except that each teacher is dealt a different deck of cards and plays a different game from other teachers in the school. All of these games require preparation and structure, however.

Successful teachers need to do lesson planning. Time is a valuable resource and deserves to be used well. Meandering one direction and another wastes time. Fifteen wasted minutes in a class of twenty-five students means 375 wasted minutes. Classes can be more interesting, help the students to learn more, and have fewer problems if they are well planned.

Most school systems offer a suggested lesson plan. It is wise for a teacher to adapt this suggested plan and use it, unless there is a serious reason to plan differently. One value in using the suggested school system lesson plan is that it ought to be specific to the goals of that community, and someone has devoted time to presenting an educationally sound plan. Another benefit in the regular use of the specified lesson plan is that it becomes natural and comfortable for the teacher to use this lesson structure when being observed on classroom visits by supervisors.

Many teachers prepare lesson plans in booklets or notebooks. The form is personal to the planner. Some teachers keep these as records of when they covered certain subjects during the school year, and they may include professional, school, and personal calendar information in the same record. Some teachers note successes or problems in their plan books also. The plans can be brief, with simple lesson topics and key words, or they can be longer and more detailed by individual choice.

A teacher should decide first *what* idea or objective is to be taught, and list that on the lesson plan. An introductory activity, which some schools call a warm-up, would be next. This allows the class to begin in an orderly manner. It should be a simple activity that students can accomplish independently, allowing the teacher to take roll and answer a few questions from individuals. Next, the teacher begins with a brief review of previous work and the checking of homework. This could be a useful time to assign the new homework, so students can note it in agenda books or notebooks.

Then an overview of the new lesson should be presented with a clear explanation of *why* this lesson is being taught. The lesson is then presented and developed. Questions on the lesson—asked of children from all areas of the classroom, boys and girls, all ethnic groups—could follow.

Closely supervised seat work or a simple hands-on project, designed to practice skills covered in the lesson, could be the next activity. Be prepared with additional interesting and challenging developmental tasks for students who finish early.

A wrap-up for closure would include a summary and evaluation of what was learned, clean-up time, and assignment or reminder of homework that reinforces the lesson. Some explanation or clarification of the homework may be needed. Be sure to end the lesson early enough to have sufficient time for the closure activities—not less than ten minutes.

Including a time schedule on the left column of the lesson plan is helpful. This will vary by subject, but seven minutes warm-up, three minutes for why of the lesson, fifteen minutes for presenting the lesson, fifteen minutes for practice skills, and five minutes for wrap-up, might be a balance for a forty-five-minute lesson.

Supplies needed for any planned project can be listed on the lesson plan. Equipment, such as a TV and VCR, can be listed, too. Clipping the lesson plan to a neon clipboard or having it easily and visually available in a notebook that is easy to find through the class period is helpful. Lesson plans can be the teacher's friend.

Respect

When one new teacher was asked what factor was most important for teachers, the answer was *respect*. If students respect the teacher, effective teaching and good discipline simply follow. The new teacher said that it was essential to be respected by other staff members, too.

Respect comes in little pieces. The way one looks at or speaks with a child or class inspires it. The appearance of self-confidence affects it. Learning students' names is important. Responses made to behaviors or words said by students develop respect. How the teacher dresses can be a factor. Stopping for a moment to ask about a new baby brother or whether a favorite sports team won can encourage respect. Working after school with cheerleaders, sports, drama groups, or clubs can win respect. Tutoring develops rapport. Correcting and returning papers in a timely manner is an element of respect. Planning interesting lessons and showing enthusiasm show respect. Strength of knowledge and capability create respect. Assuring that the classroom is comfortable and attractive is even part of respecting the students.

Some teachers, or other adults, can walk into a classroom and give an immediate image of someone who is to be respected. They may be big or tiny, tough or sweet, but students sense this security that this adult demonstrates. Many new teachers have not developed this strength. They have to work at it.

Dressing in a professional manner is important. It can be difficult to change a college student's wardrobe into a teaching wardrobe, but simple dark pants and skirts are a good beginning. Shirts, sweaters, and tops can be evaluated to find those that look most professional. Some could be topped with a jacket or vest. Dress-for-success business books suggest wearing black, navy, or dark colors for more power. This could be helpful to a new teacher.

Some students are seriously concerned about any teacher behavior that they perceive as disrespect. It is valuable to work earnestly to be polite and courteous to all students in a class. Children will be on the lookout for negative behavior from a teacher who has a different racial or cultural background. A teacher needs to recognize whether he or she is more understanding and warm toward those students who are culturally just like themselves or more gracious to boys than girls or vice versa.

Sometimes one is tempted to ignore something rude a student says. It would be stronger, and more helpful to the student, to say, "I consider that rude." Rude behavior, corrected early, is more likely to diminish. Many teachers develop a simple way to look right at a child, which causes the child to change behavior and apologize. One of the sweet things children say is "My bad" to express regret. Teachers who calmly correct small negative behaviors usually have fewer serious discipline problems. Students know well when they are disrespectful and are waiting for the correction.

Understanding a child's needs can eventually build respect. A child who one day slams books on the floor, plays with his glasses on the desk like a toy, and calls the teacher an unacceptable name may be found to have missed taking his prescribed medicine. A teacher can learn to recognize this and send the child to the health room. Listening to a disrespectful child's explanation may give the teacher enough information to work out the problem and regain the courtesy desired.

A technique that can add power and respect is to use a clipboard with paper on it. As the teacher walks about the room, notes on behavior or names can be listed on the clipboard. It does not really matter what is written on the clipboard. Some students, observing this notation, will endeavor to keep their names off the clipboard. Other teachers keep a notebook or grade book in a visible manner, noting tardiness, participation, good behavior, fights, etc., to demonstrate objectivity and to help in recalling factual information when dealing with students. Pupils with disciplinary problems can be asked to write paragraphs about improving respect and may be asked to explain the problem to parents and have them sign the paper before it is returned. Calling parents is a valuable way to gain family support for respect in the classroom. Many parents will sincerely support the teacher in this effort.

Practice talking to a group of students with a convincing tone of voice. It may help to record or videotape lessons as one works on this skill, perhaps recruiting a comfortable friend or mentor as a coach to help eliminate any whine or questioning note from teacher directions and expectations.

Staff respect may follow naturally from many of the above recommendations. A self-confident image helps with staff, too. A teacher appears stronger if he or she makes few criticisms of the school and students. It can be counterproductive to spend much time in the faculty room gossiping about students. A successful teacher is too busy and positive to do that. Time can be better spent developing some sincere relationships and friendships with teachers. Teachers can share lesson plan ideas, computer advice, discipline techniques, and valuable information about what works with a child. Respect follows spontaneously in such professional contacts. It may be wise to avoid abrasive negative staff members, whenever possible. Don't seek out persons who undermine one's feeling of self-worth.

Requesting some professional help from administration or another source is essential if a teacher believes a lack of respect to be a serious problem. The teacher does not stand alone in the classroom. The school and school system want success and respect for the teacher also. It is sad if a teacher leaves teaching out of frustration with students' disrespect. Respect can be learned and earned.

Rules the First Day of Class

Establishing classroom rules is important the first day of class. Students are most ready to establish an impression of the teacher and what is expected at the beginning. In this way, no time and emotions are wasted correcting students before the teacher gets a chance to fairly state his or her expectations.

Every teacher establishes certain important rules. A simple five-step rule list can be made, or detailed longer lists of rules can be presented. The rules can result from collaboration with students or be created entirely by the teacher. Or there could be a combination of student rules plus teacher's rules.

The choice of how to formulate rules may depend on how much time the teacher decides to spend on this activity. If students are to be involved in creating the rules list, it will take more time. Students will often come up with a list of familiar and useful rules and may understand and cooperate more fully with rules they had a part in making. On the other hand, simply using a teacher-driven list of rules is quicker and will allow more early class time for other activities the teacher has planned. Each teacher weighs these factors and decides how to proceed to present rules for class behavior.

Many variations of creating a rules list will work. It is the value and follow-through placed on the rules, plus the early timing, which bring successful classroom management.

An example of a Five-Point Expectation List is:

1. Respect all persons in this classroom
2. Sit in your seat
3. Begin work right away
4. Quietly work
5. Clean up quickly

Learn Names

A child responds swiftly to his or her name. This is a key element in working with any child. It is essential to call on a child by name. Correcting behavior, giving earned praise, greeting in the hallway, recording work, identifying a child in faculty discussions about students, all require the teacher to use the students' names.

Some teachers learn names with ease. Some work at it and pride themselves on this skill. Others find it difficult, particularly with large classes, and those which change by the hour, and also by the quarter or semester. Techniques that help with remembering names include placement of students in regular or assigned seats. Then the teacher can use a seating chart until names are learned. Some teachers need the seating chart for a very long time, but it still affords the teacher a method to use to call a child by name. Some teachers try to associate names with a special characteristic of a child. This can be enhanced the first day of class with a name association game. Each child could name a food or animal that begins with the same letter as the child's name. Another association could be to name a favorite Beanie Baby, football team, etc.

Many teachers have students make up name tags to wear or have them fold index cards lengthwise, write their names on the cards, and tape them to each student's desk as an aid in learning and using names. Some teachers set up the names on the top of desks before the children enter the room, to assign seats and remind the teacher, and other students, of names. It is beneficial for classroom bonding and friendships to post names for all to learn.

On the first day of class, when students respond to the roll call, a teacher can invite students to teach the teacher how to pronounce their names. The teacher can write this phonetically in the grade book and on the seating chart for a reminder when speaking the name. An example of a phonetic cue would be (MEL-on-nee) for Melanie or (en-DAY-jah) for Endeja or (cor-TREES) for Cortress.

Many students dislike hearing their names mispronounced. This creates a barrier between the teacher and the student.

The use of names is a powerful tool for the teacher and builds rapport with students. It deserves serious attention and effort. If it is simply not possible to learn all the names, be sure to use a seating chart to achieve the ability to at least *use* the students' names. Teachers develop more security and satisfaction when they can name their students.

 ## Grade Record

Setting up a grade record for each class as early in the grading period as possible will make grading of students easier and more valid. The school system may require a particular record book or computer program. Teachers use a wide variety of books, some small, some large. It is valuable to have some type of loose-leaf book, so pages can be added or taken out. Pages can then be added if the teacher finds there are more grades to enter than anticipated. Occasionally, a record page can be damaged and need replacement. Water could be spilled across the page, for example, or a student could bleed or drop ink on the page; many unanticipated things happen in school classes.

Promptly starting the grade record allows the teacher to enter several grades for each child early in the grading period. A teacher can then easily begin to recognize which children need extra help and which ones are doing so well that they can benefit from enhanced lessons. A teacher will be asked for reports on individual student's work early in the period and will need these records. Putting off entering grades from student work and papers during the first part of the grading period leaves a record-entering task that can be tedious or simply never done. Experienced teachers know to enter grades quickly and keep up with that task.

The record book should have a title page for entering the name of teacher, school name, classroom number, time period, and grade or class identification. This is also a good place to list a grading key, briefly explaining what a number or letter grade, star, slash, zero, plus, minus, colored dot, or any other symbol represents. Some school systems require the teacher to turn in grade records at the end of the school year, so these notations are essential.

The teacher should identify each page of the grade record, listing the class name, class hour, and date of initiation and end of the recording period. Along the left side, student names are listed, generally in alphabetical order. Since it is recommended that this grade record be started as soon as possible, new student names may have to be added at the end. These will not be alphabetical and may cause some location problems for the teacher. However, starting the record before all information can be perfect has more benefits to outweigh this problem. Teachers learn to print this information as neatly as possible. Some note pronunciation cues near each name.

At the top of the grade record, there is usually space to list each graded item by date and brief identification, such as Quiz 1 or Adverbs. Diligence in immediately entering a title for each column of grades is a habit that will pay off in easier future interpretation of work completed. It also helps when make-up work needs to be listed for that assignment. During conferences, parents often demand specifics about grades for individual assignments.

It may be helpful to enter grades in pencil. This allows teachers to correct mistakes and may speed the process. An experienced teacher can recognize grades he or she entered and would spot any changes a student might make. The grade record should stay out of students' hands, of course, which will prevent any alterations.

Most teachers nowadays will want to enter grades in the computer. Some will wish a back-up hard-copy record book, as described above. Two records can add a lot of work, however, so you may prefer to use only the computer. If you are faithful in saving every entry list to a floppy disk, in addition to the computer hard disk record, there should be no problem with lost grades.

The benefits of computer-recorded grades are many. For one thing, the lists of names can be kept alphabetized. The records can be printed out for several purposes. Grades can be added and averaged by the computer (this is the biggest benefit). Grading factors, such as 25% for quizzes and tests, etc., can be factored into the final grade automatically. The computer's mail-merge function can be used for letters to students or parents, telling of grade or behavior status. These letters can be personalized with names, grades, and even addresses for each child.

Some teachers use special simplified computer programs, such as Teacher Toolbox, for recording grades. Most teachers, even those who consider themselves almost computer-illiterate, could enter class identification, date of assignment, name titles, assignment titles, and summary titles into a regular computer program, such as Office or Clarisworks. They then create a spreadsheet, entering student names and scores. These skills can be learned by a teacher in about four hours. Most schools have a person or workshop class available to help teachers learn these skills. With this help, the teacher could create a floppy disk to use as an example for setting up all classes. It is best to keep the floppy disk example, unchanged, and simply use it by copying it each time.

Some of the more advanced skills, such as entering formulas into the database and creating a merge letter, would require more computer lessons.

Grading

Grading is not something experienced teachers do only at the end of the quarter. The time to begin grading is the first day of class. It is important that a student understands how he or she will be graded.

A clear grading policy can be distributed or explained the first day of class. It is part of the expectations the teacher presents to the new class. Students do not seem to carry assumptions about grading from class to class. There is a need for every teacher to be specific to the class taught.

A possible grading policy could include:

25% - for quizzes and tests
10% - for homework
35% - for daily work
20% - for special projects and reports
10% - for work habits
100% - total grade

Each lesson can begin with a simple explanation of grading for that segment. This can be done with points, a rubric, a grading scale, or any standard set by the teacher. It is worthwhile to write this on the blackboard, overhead projector, or cards, so students who are visual learners will understand better.

Make-up work is a separate expectation to be explained by the teacher. Make-up work is often a difficult concept for a student to comprehend. The student is not generally very aware that work went on in the classroom while he or she was absent. This is particularly true if the student has fulfilled the school's attendance policy. Students who have excused absences often believe they are also excused from the work done for the excused period. The teacher needs to make it very clear that work is to be done for make up and turned in.

Locating and explaining make-up work can be very trying for a teacher. Some teachers give make-up work that is the same as what the class did. Others have special make-up assignments. A number of teachers assign students partners who are responsible for getting make-up work to the missing child. The student can ask another student who lives nearby to bring home make-up work if the student knows in advance the day will be missed. The student can also ask the teacher for make-up work before or after the absence. Make-up assignments can be located in a special section of the room for returning students to find their own missed work. To develop responsibility and really give students a fair chance to be graded as highly as those who were in attendance every day, a teacher should work out one of these systems, or a combination of them, that allows for consistent opportunity for students to make up work. The teacher needs to explain the chosen system clearly and repeat it from time to time.

Students often believe the report card grade they will receive is higher than what is supported by the teacher's record. These students do not factor in work not completed and quickly forget poor grades on some work. They tend to keep only "A" papers and good work. It is valuable to allow students to average their grades for themselves, or at least for the teacher to explain to them that three high grades and three missing grades will equal a low grade.

Grading problems sometimes come back to haunt teachers when report card grades are given. However, students who understand their grade rarely complain. They can also generally explain the grade to a parent who was hoping for a higher grade. Clearly explained grading factors, repeated several times during a grading period, can prevent many parent conferences from turning hostile. When a teacher is asked to explain the grade during a parent conference, it can be done objectively, with no reason for the teacher to be defensive or nervous.

Grades are important to students, parents, and teachers. They form a framework for teaching and evaluating. Teachers can sometimes reflect on class grades to determine their effectiveness, fairness, and satisfactions with teaching accomplishments.

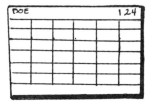

Seating Chart

The second day of class is an optimum time for assigning seats to the students, using a seating chart. During the first day of class, the teacher can make quick notes on the roll sheet to indicate behavior with a plus or minus (or even two minuses). Maybe the teacher can make quick notes that someone is successful (or not) near another student, needs to be nearer the teacher for control or a physical need, etc.

Asking students to fill out cards or information sheets on the first day is also helpful for creating this seating chart. Students can note health problems, particularly for seeing the board or hearing the teacher. If one lists asthma as a problem, that child might benefit from a seat on the outside edge of the group, where it is more peaceful and more air space is provided. Students could also be invited to choose a friend to sit at the same table, if the teacher divides the class into teams this way. Friends should be seated across the table from each other, however, not next to each other where too much conversation is likely to ensue and become disruptive. Some teachers will also want to mix up boys and girls and structure some ethnic mix in the classroom.

The teacher should have the completed seating chart ready when students arrive the second day. After a quieting beginning activity, assigning the new seats should be the next priority. Expect the movement of children to new seats to be a bit noisy. Students take a few minutes to adjust to this new seating, but rarely complain. Write down any complaints or problems noticed as the day progresses. Take time to think through carefully whether you wish to change the students. Change only a serious problem right away.

The value of the seating chart is that it gives the teacher stronger control of the classroom. Students know the teacher is responsible for where they sit. Disruptive students are generally cooperative in moving to another location for successful discipline when *the teacher has assigned the seats in the first place*. It can prevent a power struggle all quarter or year. Moving students to different seats can be one of the few techniques the teacher will need to use to control noise, touching, copying, or other unwanted behavior in the classroom.

Chapter 2

ഇ൦ങ

Rapport with Students

Child-Centered Classes

Students greet the teacher as they enter the classroom. The teacher greets the students by name. Several gather at the teacher's desk while attendance is taken. Most begin working quietly, in their seats, on a warm-up assignment. Immediately, the teacher is immersed in student-driven needs. One raises a hand to ask a question about the assignment, while the teacher is still dealing with another student's concerns at the desk. Across the room, two children become restless and may need teacher intervention.

Teachers can learn to stare down the restless ones, ask the one with hand up to wait just a minute, and complete the ongoing conversation. Calm, patient teachers handle pressure from different directions regularly. Setting priorities and understanding that the child is the focus of the class drives the teacher's response to student requests and demands.

An exception to this basic rule that the class be child-centered is that the class must stay orderly for safety and for education to take place. Sometimes the teacher must respond to conflict or noise before proceeding to any other matter. Orderly classrooms are a foundation for teaching. Teachers tolerate different noise levels, but anyone can recognize a disrespectful, disorderly class. That needs to be set right with management skills immediately. Disruption can also be prevented by training the group to begin work on their own at the beginning of classes. It is realistic to expect a short period of social interaction and sounds of children settling themselves and books as the class assembles and sits down. Then the class should get down to productive business.

After initial critical needs are met, a teacher can present the lesson. The lesson should involve varying techniques benefiting children with different learning styles. Sadly, this is not always true. Teachers tend to teach to their own learning styles for personal comfort. Thus, some teachers always lecture, some always show long films so they can sit back and relax, and some assign long writing assignments to force class quiet and provide the teacher a peaceful time to correct papers or read. Certain teachers do not prepare much in the way of lesson plans, preferring to "teach off the cuff." Their classes may not move through much of the curriculum during the grading period. It is sad to waste students' time in that way, because a wasted half-hour is really twelve wasted hours for twenty-four students.

Children like activity, so some student movement should be planned into the lesson. It could be working with manipulative items, such as rulers, protractors, microscopes, maps and colored pencils, bridge construction materials, etc. Or it could be a cooperative project to produce a short play, conduct a science experiment, prepare a salad, or create a large chart of brainstorming ideas on class behavior rules for school assemblies. Child-focused classes often spend some time making special projects. It is important that each activity chosen is part of the lesson plan and has a direct correlation to the teaching objectives.

Teachers who ignore this need of children for activity often do this to avoid disruption. It takes planning to have the necessary materials and supplies readily available and to instill accountability from the outset of the task. Activity requires alert discipline on the part of the teacher, who should have prepared the children with clear rules for them to follow. A calm manner of expecting good behavior is also a requirement for successful activity lessons.

In a child-centered class, the teacher encourages participation from all students, being careful to listen to, and call on, girls, boys, and children of all ethnic backgrounds and ability levels. Modifying the curriculum to meet individual student needs shows child focus, too. The teacher should make these adaptations to the best of his or her ability and consider the time allowed. The teacher may help some reluctant students get started, encourage certain children, and isolate others as part of this individualizing.

Certain teachers work with an intimidation system. They attempt to be so strict, threatening, and gruff that children fear to speak up in their classes. But school is intended to be a place to seek, find, and learn answers for life. Absolutely quiet, *threatened* children miss a great deal.

On the other hand, some instructors try so hard to be friends or pals with their students that teaching time gets wasted, too. Rapport and understanding of individual pupils and needs is important, but these teachers sometimes go too far, forgetting that an instructor-student relationship requires a mentoring role, not a buddy one.

Concentrating on the child means trying to get the room as comfortable as possible. The room may be too cold. A window blind may be broken and cannot be lowered. Lights may be burned out. These can require repeated requests and follow-ups to custodians and administration. Do not give up. A child needs a degree of comfort to learn.

Listening and alert observation are essential for teachers. Teachers in child-centered classes attempt to welcome student questions and observations, listening carefully to what is said and responding with care. Looking a child in the eyes when he or she is telling something, patiently asking the child to repeat or explain more clearly, and responding to what was said are examples of good listening skills. Observing student frustration, noting a student who is not beginning to work, and circling the room to be in close proximity of each child for periods of time are examples of alert observation.

A student-focused teacher stays aware of the child's world. It helps to keep up with some of the sports teams, music groups, books, fads, clothing styles, TV shows, and movies that are popular with the children, and to be aware of their activity group participation, special awards, and recognition. Sometimes it is appropriate to know about family problems, health problems, and certainly special needs of the students. Each of these areas requires sincerity and a lack of put-downs and judgments.

Courteous respect should be given to the students with regard to assigning homework and scheduling tests, with an understanding of the children's total school program. It is considerate to assign few or no homework assignments to be completed on weekends. It may be more successful to assign homework at the beginning of the class. If not, be sure to allow enough time at the end of class to make the assignment clear. Teachers can ask students whether a scheduled test falls on the same day as other tests. Perhaps an alternate time can be set, if the teacher is flexible. A thoughtful teacher will allow several days' notice before large assignments are due.

Sometimes teachers and school staff members need to remind themselves that the child is the focus of the school. Convenience for adults and ease of the working situation are not primary. Children are the business and the product of a school. Good education recognizes this priority.

Smiles

Smiles are controversial in teaching. Some teachers don't smile until October. Some never smile. Smiling is a personal choice for a teacher. Students like smiles and most say they wish their teachers smiled more.

Hopefully a teacher has chosen this field of work because he or she enjoys children. A natural and comfortable part of communicating with children is to smile and laugh with them. Smiling relaxes both the teacher and the students. It can make a teacher tense to be frowning all the time or sternly expressing disapproval with a frozen face. Stress is relieved by relaxing and smiling as one greets students, takes roll, explains lessons, listens to reports, observes and guides work on projects, and evaluates the tasks orally.

Creating a quiet, serene, pleasant, nonthreatening climate in a classroom should be a goal for teaching. Calming students and keeping them on the job can make each class more productive. The positive teacher may have fewer students who are afraid to tackle the assignment. Being pleasant builds rapport with students. A teacher can practice smiling to develop this.

Smiling at natural opportunities does not mean the teacher is not being firm with the class. The right balance might be explained as "tender authority." The teacher is in charge and will respond to problems with a strong, clear voice. Teachers are not pals and need not bargain with students for fewer questions to answer, opportunities to change seats, etc. Students will soon learn that this teacher is steadfast and anticipates cooperation.

Disciplining students, or a whole class, is naturally *not* done with a smile. These are times for a total manner of strength and image of disapproval. It is important to appear and sound objective, referring to the situation. The main message to convey is that "I dislike this behavior, though I still like you." The teacher should clearly explain what was inappropriate and attempt to modify the behavior. When all has returned to a calm classroom climate, the teacher, and the students, can relax and smile again.

Each teacher needs to balance the firm projection of strength with relaxed, smiling teaching times. Obviously, there is a kernel to learn from the teachers who do not smile until October. Most teachers need to emphasize the firm, in-charge image the first day and over the first weeks. Restless classes may make a strong, unsmiling teacher's face a necessity. A goal will be to create the relaxed classroom that allows students and teacher to smile together and enjoy education.

Eye Contact

 Eye contact can be an important element of inter-action in a classroom. Teachers who speak directly to their students while holding eye contact are very effective. Sometimes college speech class students are told to look over the heads of the audience if they are nervous. This is a poor technique in a classroom, however. Some teachers tend to look mainly at the restless students or those who are particularly eager to answer questions. The teacher should try to develop a practice of scanning the faces of each of the students, perhaps working from the back of the class to the front, as he or she is developing a point of the lesson. This leads the students to concentrate on the meaning of what the teacher is saying.

Sincere eye contact is part of the development of rapport between teacher and student. It is particularly important to look directly at students in personal interchanges. This can help the teacher determine whether the student understands what was said and can lend strength to the message. Objective eye contact is essential when disciplining a student.

Students should be coached to raise their hands before speaking so the teacher can direct some questions to quiet, shy students who would otherwise be overlooked and ignored. Eye contact is important when a teacher is practicing "wait time" to give a child sufficient time to formulate and come forth with an answer. This watch-and-wait time can seem long to the teacher and the class, but it is needed to get participation from many students, especially shy ones, some girls, and some minority students.

It is valuable to gain eye contact from the group of students. Teachers can facilitate this by discouraging distractions. Turning off or covering an overhead projector screen will help students focus on the teacher instead of the bright light. Turning off a film or video or music to make a point is a similar technique. Distractions in the classroom, such as restless students, fan noises, loud hallway noises, etc., may need to be dealt with before continuing with the teaching message.

Teachers like individual students to make eye contact with them. This is a positive factor for rapport and reception of the message. However, in certain cultural backgrounds, eye contact is not encouraged and is considered disrespectful, so the teacher is wise not to push this point with some students who choose not to make eye contact.

Some teachers believe that the way they dress makes them more appealing to students to look at. Some purposely wear bright colors. Others believe that students think a teacher wearing dark colors is stronger and will give them more respect. Some like to dress attractively or in a businesslike manner to gain visual attention. Some people believe that teaching is a performing art. This is why certain teachers use gestures and facial movements to keep the children's attention. Students like to look at a smiling teacher.

Ethnic Difference

Teachers can suffer self-doubt when they consider ethnic diversity in their classrooms. Some think they would be more successful with certain students if they were of the same cultural background. However, the world is full of real-life situations with people of mixed cultures. Teachers can work well with children who are different from them. Their students benefit from this successful interaction for the life goals that lie ahead.

Some research seems to indicate that teachers *are* more effective with students of the same ethnic background. Certain school systems in Baltimore, Minneapolis, Detroit, Milwaukee, New York City, and elsewhere have experimented with such programs. No one has discovered "the right answer" to this subject. Schools are still struggling with "at risk" students with lagging achievement.

Despite these educational struggles, the teacher still wants to succeed with all the students assigned to his or her classes and therefore needs to focus on these sensitive factors. Many of these factors depend upon self-reflection, studying students and their cultures, and being willing to empathize and understand. The teacher displays these attitudes from the first moment of interaction with students. Students can detect quickly whether you like them. There are invisible antennae that sense this, even in the youngest of children.

One of the prime factors is supreme courtesy. Students deserve to hear a teacher say please, thank you, do you wish? would you like to? Children want to hear a pleasant tone of voice. They want to see smiles and cheerfulness. One of the biggest complaints of a student who is angry often is that the student was rudely spoken to or disrespected. Some teachers unconsciously are more courteous and sweet speaking to children of the teacher's own ethnic background. One way to recognize this problem is to tape-record a question-and-answer classroom lesson, being sure to use names to identify which child is being spoken to. Listen for voice changes when the tape is played back.

There is a fine line between sincere politeness and paternalism. Paternalistic teachers use condescending terms like, "Dearie" as they communicate with students. These children get the clear impression the teacher knows he or she is smarter and more valuable. Phrases, such as "you people" or "your kind" and comments like "This is the way educated people do it" carry a paternalistic message. The child picks up that he or she is not rated as highly as the teacher. Another way teachers indicate lower respect for one group of students is to lower expectations of them for gum chewing, wearing hats, attitude, etc. It also helps to loan pencils, pens, and paper with some check-out procedure, without scorn. The teacher needs to practice an objective approach and avoid appearing too benevolent.

Another way children pick up on a lack of ethnic fairness is when a teacher calls on students of one ethnic group more than others. Sometimes it is obvious that the teacher gives more desirable questions to some children. The sensitive teacher tries to call on *all* class members equally. This means boys and girls, students at the back and front of the room, and certainly children of all ethnic backgrounds. Most teachers need to consciously focus on this need. Calling on children with an organized plan takes top-level concentration and requires classroom management to keep certain dominating students listening and patient. This is a *crucial* point for developing all students' self-esteem, especially that of withholding and insecure students, who will need a good deal of classroom "wait time." The sensitive teacher will recognize the satisfaction these reluctant participants gain from successfully answering.

The sharp teacher can mentally keep track of the whole classroom and eventually call on *every* student. This will insure that children of all ethnic backgrounds are heard. It may be helpful for the teacher to keep a class list or use a section of the grade book, checking off names as each child is called on. Some teachers benefit by using the seating chart, as they endeavor to call on every child, waiting long enough for each child to answer.

Passive children require sensitive approaches. Sometimes these students are left out unconsciously by a teacher, who may not understand their culture. It is of benefit to encourage eye contact, but don't require it. Some families teach their children that keeping one's eyes cast down shows respect. Gently drawing out these students, encouraging their participation in class activities, promotes ethnic fairness. These students will appreciate the nonpressured reassurance.

Teachers think some students are too noisy. Loud voices can have social, family, cultural and physical factors. One of the easiest ways to deal with noise is simply to wait a few minutes at the beginning of the class until the volume dies down. Early criticism of the behavior of these students can be interpreted as ethnic disapproval. Getting the group immediately started on an easy-to-understand assignment can also be helpful. Teachers use noise-lowering signals throughout their classes. Moving toward a chattering group will usually quiet them down. Students will be quieter when they are highly motivated to the task they are doing.

Concerned teachers are interested in sports and able to discuss them with children. They go to school games and notice players' moves, skills, and successes. They also attend choral, band, art, and science programs. Demonstrating sincere interest in soccer, football, basketball, music, etc. can forge a cross-ethnic communication and bond with students. Sensitive instructors notice students' hairstyles, clothes choices, and new shoes, enjoying their trend-setting and diversity. One should not be judgmental about these culturally affected personal choices of students.

Use care in seating arrangements. It can prevent many problems to consider the ethnic make-up of the class and assign seats with some mix. Choose leaders and helpers to reflect the composition of the class. Evaluate your discipline procedures from time to time to determine whether you are fair to all students. Students will work in class if they like and trust the teacher. Otherwise they will show their anger or distaste by not working.

Teachers who work with diverse children can benefit by exposure to varied cultural events in music, dance, theater, television, movies, and social occasions. Listen to advice from educational workshops and colleagues. Be a strong, positive, capable person. Never give up.

Accent the Positive

You can do it! What do you like best about this picture? That is an important point. I like the way you kept working on the problem until you knew you had the right answer. I admire the way you tried to figure out the answer yourself, before you asked for help. Nice going! Excellent! I knew you could do it.

These are some of the hundreds of ways teachers have to encourage their students. Children respond and learn enormously more with favorable messages rather than heavy criticism. This positive teaching starts at the beginning of class and continues throughout the period. It is not merely a practice of saying things in a positive way to kids; it also includes how material is presented and the attitude of the teacher.

When the class begins, an enthusiastic teacher introduces the lesson, explaining why students are learning this material. An attempt will have been made to choose interesting teaching techniques that children enjoy and react to well. Children's responses are sharply observed by the teacher. The teacher moves toward a noisy or restless group or child. If this does not change behavior, the teacher may ask someone in that group what one already knows about the topic. This focuses students to the task at hand. Then the teacher may be able to tie these children's thoughts into the lesson.

The teacher may notice an inattentive student next. Again, the teacher moves toward the child. Helping the child get on task could mean assisting him or her with finding a page, getting out paper and pencil, or even writing a title or first sentence the child has volunteered. This teacher might need repeated trips back to keep the child focused.

Even positive teachers correct behavior. An objective, firm command is made to "Stop fighting," as teacher moves near. "Crayons are to be carefully handled, not broken." *Positive* never means push-over. A teacher maintains a directed, organized classroom climate, but does so in a nonthreatening, clearly explained manner.

Positive educators are often heard to say "I like the quiet way all of you are working" or "This class behavior pleases me" when the whole class is industriously working. Students enjoy teacher appreciation and kind words.

As the lesson proceeds, students like to be given notice that the activity will change in a few minutes. This gives them time to finish a thought process, problem, or page. It also affords them an opportunity to shift mindset to the change. It is beneficial not to confront children with change in a dogmatic manner.

Clear transition messages help students, too. "It is time to close your books, put them under your desk, and open your notebook to your social studies section." Or "Box up your colored pencils carefully, return them to the pencil basket, and join the music circle quietly." These messages organize the children for cooperation. Students will remind each other of the clear instructions, aiding the teacher's task.

Give a moment of quiet before beginning a new lesson element. Make sure all students are settled and quiet. Use management skills, if necessary at this point, because breakdown of class attention is common at this point, affected by this change and continuing time spent in this one location. It doesn't pay to proceed until the group is ready. Students and teacher become a bit more tired as the class moves along and patience is required to avoid grumpiness and negative behavior from children and teacher. Students need to be reminded of how this sequence relates to the stated lesson objectives.

Near the end of a class is a valuable time to strengthen positive thoughts. You can ask students what they learned and accomplished. The teacher can reinforce the planned objectives. Enough time to make this summary meaningful should be allowed. One very successful teacher often said at the end of a class, "We enjoyed this class and learned a lot today," giving the children a sincere smile. Hopefully positive teachers and their students will agree with this assessment.

Incidents happen regularly during a class session. If a child tips over a small vase of flowers on the teacher's desk, for example, the teacher can hand him or her a sponge and simply move items to another place. This allows the child an opportunity to redeem himself or herself and breathe a sigh of relief that there was no scolding.

Teachers who accent the positive sincerely enjoy children. Students know this immediately and respond to this. You can teach so much more powerfully with positive messages than with negative, intimidating ones.

The Word "But"

The word *but* is so small, but it can make a real difference when a teacher gives a comment to a student. The entire message is changed if the word *but* is added to what the teacher says. This is a word that could be consciously deleted from the teacher's vocabulary.

Perhaps a child has just finished an drawing of snow in a tree. The teacher might make the comment, "Your tree is so natural and I can see the careful placement of snow on flat parts of branches, *but* your tree is pretty green for mid-winter." What part of that statement—meant to express earned praise—did the student hear? The child most likely focuses on the thought, "The teacher thinks my tree is too green," and never really hears the praise of the natural-looking tree and careful placement of snow. This evaluation becomes a negative one, in effect.

People hear about 95 percent positive comments about themselves each day. But they usually focus most on the 5 percent of negative observations they hear. We worry and fret over these details. This is expressed in the cliche "You don't see the forest for the trees."

We can aid children, in positive evaluation, by phasing out the word *but* when describing their behavior or work. Consider the statement, "You have been quiet in class today, *but* I wish you would sit up and not be so sloppy in your chair." The child, hearing this, will interpret it as just another criticism. The listener usually misses the first positive comment entirely. The same point could be made if the teacher said, "You have been quiet in class today. Now let's work on sitting up with on-task posture in your chair." The child has a chance to swallow and believe the compliment about quiet behavior. The next point is not hooked to the praise. It would be stronger praise yet if said alone, with sitting behavior corrected at another time.

The word *but* can be confusing in lesson instructions also. It is better to give simple, clear directions, leaving out as many *but* connectors as possible. Here's an example of confusing instructions: "Choose a world leader to research and write a report on, *but* do not choose the same one everyone always chooses. Check with the librarian for advice, if needed with your choice. Read at least three references, *but* do not just copy them from the Internet. Write at least five paragraphs about your leader, *but* do not double-space them. Make sure every paragraph tells a fact, with supporting details about that fact, *but* not confusing items not related to that fact."

Leaving out the word *but* clarifies the instructions: "Choose a world leader to research and write a report on. Do not choose the same one everyone always chooses. Check with the librarian for advice, if needed with your choice. Read at least three references. Do not just copy them from the Internet. Write at least five paragraphs about your leader. Single-space them. Make sure every paragraph tells a fact, with supporting details about that fact. Check each paragraph to eliminate confusing items not related to that fact."

Teaching without the word *but* aids a class in focusing on the instruction. It helps individual students to receive an earned positive compliment or comment with enjoyment. It adds sharpness to instruction. And it will enhance the teacher's rapport with pupils. Teachers can practice developing this skill. Some may wish to tape-record a class session to study how they are presently dealing with this element of teaching.

Flexibility

Every day is different in teaching. Wise teachers form lesson plans for every day and create strategies for units and yearly goals. However, the students entering the classroom are not a static group. Their needs vary day by day. Individual students have strong demands on the day's interaction. Some students, especially in early morning classes, can be extremely passive and sleepy (unless they have experienced an active and social bus ride to school). Sometimes whole classes entering the class following recess, a program, physical education class, or lunch are very physical and excited. Students at the end of the day can be tired, restless, and disinterested. Endless factors affect students' moods. Great excitement arises, for example, if they see snow falling outside the window. Rain can make them worry about their trips home. A fight or an agitated student can upset the others. Lack of supplies or equipment can discourage them. Many varieties of perceived skill insecurities by students may create difficult teaching situations. Noise, too much heat or cold, and too little light can also affect an educational climate. Resistance to a new teacher would be another factor to consider.

The successful teacher will try to adapt the intended lesson for this volatile classroom world. Flexibility, applied with calmness, is essential. It becomes natural and almost automatic to adjust tone of voice, lesson directions, strength of discipline, timing of the lesson, and similar factors to respond to the perceived needs of the class or a student.

The quiet, early-morning group may need a gentle, motivating approach. There could be more need to stimulate work and check that students are on task. Some students may be slow starters at this time of day. It becomes a problem for the others, and for the teacher, when work is not completed or the class is delayed for the slow starters to catch up.

The class that enters the room excited and agitated from physical education or lunch, requires a calming approach from the teacher, given with a sense of humor and a smile. A teacher needs to remember what it was like to have fun and be elated at that age. This is an appropriate time to allow a slower beginning for class, so the animation can simmer down a bit on its own. However, when the teacher determines that enough time has been given and sees that the class has taken on a quieter tone, it is time to clearly state, with a voice that carries conviction, "I am ready to begin." When the class is completely quiet, the teacher gives clear, firm directions for the group. Teachers may need to use hand signals or other techniques to get the class quiet. It is essential to gain quiet class attention in this situation to gain student respect and to begin an effective lesson. Students will be responsive to the need for order if the teacher sincerely expects it.

The afternoon classes, when the children are tired, can be a challenge for a teacher, who may also be tired. Teachers are wise to learn to conserve energy throughout the day. Making sure to eat and choosing food that does not make one sleepy are important. Limiting sweets and caffeine can also be beneficial. Teacher techniques to avoid fatigue during the day include using stools or chairs at appropriate times, controlling high emotions such as anger and frustration, and simplifying and pacing some lessons. The later classes may need more animated motivation from the teacher. Focusing on making the lesson interesting with hands-on projects, *short* films or videos, visual presentations, computer activities, and cooperative learning projects could get students on task and involved, rather than sitting passively.

Teachers are always called upon to respond to individual student's needs. The students who need supplies need supplies, not a lecture. Some teachers sell pencils; some write a note about the student's supply need in a student agenda book or on a piece of paper for a parent to sign. Sometimes there is a procedure at school for aiding students who need supplies. Some students may need to be told the hours and availability of an in-school store. Ultimately, the student needs the supply item, so the teacher may have to provide it. Teachers can work out reward systems to motivate students to bring supplies and books, if this becomes a problem. Teachers can compliment students for providing the supplies they need. The positive value of being prepared can be demonstrated by providing lessons using the materials in a manner that the student recognizes as important. When a teacher gives higher marks for full use of all supplies, the student understands that using the supplies brings visible results.

Insecure students will respond to positive teaching techniques. Modifying or simplifying the lesson may help some students. It may help to put a heading on a child's paper, discuss the assignment, and write the first sentence for the child. This child may need several return trips for encouragement. Lesson instructions may need repetition or the display of examples of previous work. Some students would prefer to tuck themselves into a quiet location to work alone, with less distraction. An expectation on the teacher's part that all students will work will be perceived by the class.

Flexibility is needed if the weather changes abruptly, also. Watching a fresh snowfall can be allowed, for a moment of pleasure, but it is usually more successful to be firm about students' staying in their seats and moving on with their work. Of course, some will naturally return their attention to the window view, but a whole class rushing to the window is disruptive and difficult to control. Most students are familiar enough with classroom structure from their previous teachers to preserve order. If there is a moment of chaos, however, the teacher needs to move toward the students and give them strong, calm direction to return to assigned seats. If all else fails, the blinds can be gently let down.

It is trying for students and teachers to have to adapt to uncomfortable classrooms. It is essential for the teacher to seek an improvement for these situations. Noise, temperature, and light problems require requests for custodial or administrative help. It is valuable to write up the requests for these busy people. One may also need to remind them personally. Do keep following up on the requests, courteously and patiently, until they are accomplished. Many teachers give up or are not consistent with follow-up until the work is done.

The ever-changing atmosphere of a classroom requires a creative and self-confident teacher. It helps to project the image of a firm, calm teacher who can handle the varying aspects of the students and the school program.

Chapter 3

ॐ

Classroom Management

Structure

Students respond to a basic structure for classroom activity set by the teacher. The teacher creates a plan before children ever arrive in the classroom. This builds a foundation of rules and expectations. Some teachers then develop additional rules and standards with the students, modifying the original plan. This interaction with children builds the walls of the structure. The teacher must make sure students understand what is expected of them. Throughout the grading period, the teacher's *consistency* at enforcing the structure standards is something like the flying buttresses on a medieval church that support the building. This means reminding, repeating, and encouraging compliance with the rules throughout the school period. Don't make the mistake of going too far in befriending the children. Remember, the instructor is the authority figure, right from the start, and must be consistent with discipline and following rules. Just work at getting students to follow procedures at the first part of a school period.

Lack of consistency chips away at structure. If respect for each other is a basic rule of the class, the teacher needs to be alert and listen to what children are saying to each other and observe the attitudes they display to teachers. Each example of disrespect needs response and modification of behavior. It is worth stopping the class to deal with the situation. If possible, give the class a short assignment and confer with the disrespectful student in the hallway or in a fairly private corner of the room. A child can be moved to a seat a slight distance from other children if the matter is not resolved.

A child who does not take an assigned seat or moves inappropriately about the classroom cues the teacher to move toward the child and state objectively, "It is time to be seated in assigned seats." Firm repetition may be necessary, using the same words as is explained in the section of this book titled, "The Broken Record." A private conference, as suggested above, may be needed. One teacher tried delineating an area around a problem child's desk with masking tape on the floor to clearly show the child his limited movement area. The tape worked and that child stayed in the area, not disturbing others.

If poor work habits and attention to task is the problem, think through the scope of the lack of industry. When only one or two children are uncooperative, work with them one-on-one, preferably privately. If a certain group is not participating, separate and reseat these students. If the whole class seems disinterested, re-evaluate the lesson plan. If the material simply must be covered, such as multiplication tables, take more time to explain why students need to learn this topic. Allow a couple of students to explain briefly why they find the topic interesting and how they learn it. Become a bit of a cheerleader and stir enthusiasm, if possible. There are many incentives one can offer: names or stars on charts, certificates of completion, extra recess or computer time, etc.

When the class is not quiet enough to proceed in an orderly manner, don't proceed. Wait for quiet, using a signal system, if appropriate. A class that continues to be noisy may need a change to a written assignment, which may quiet the group. An example of a quick written assignment would be to ask students to alphabetize a readily available list of words. When most students complete this assignment and the group is quiet, collect the papers and return to the previous lesson sequence. Expect the class to begin quietly at this point.

Clean-up can be a problem. Make sure there is enough time allowed for this task. If giving more time does not improve cooperation, consider offering an incentive for the row or table that finishes and is back in order first. This contest requires *alertness* to guarantee fairness in choosing the winning group. The teacher may avoid being challenged as a referee by stating the rule at the onset as, "The first group *I see* cleaned up and in order, wins."

Each element of structure creates work for the teacher to sustain. The framework of rules and procedures will collapse if the teacher does not *consistently* support and endorse them. The teacher is the flying buttress to keep the structure standing.

Maintain as simple a structure as possible. This is the element experienced teachers understand. They know which areas and rules are important. New teachers can spend too much time with charts of behavior, tickets for positive actions (see chapter 8), scolding lectures, and consequence assignments. A teacher can spend hours on paperwork for some of these techniques. Think this through carefully when planning for creating the strong classroom climate. Choose only those items you enthusiastically support and can *consistently* sustain.

If a time comes when a teacher reassesses the success of a procedure and finds it is not working well, the teacher should try a new rule. It may be wise to discuss this problem with a supervisor or mentor to gain insights into what may work better. Once the new plan is made, explain briefly to the students why the change is being made and clearly teach the new procedure. Special care needs to be taken to faithfully reinforce the students' compliance with this new structural element.

Recognizing when a student or group of students is doing well is an essential part of structure. Children need to know when their behavior is appropriate. This teacher recognition reinforces the strong positive structure of the class.

Responsibility

Responsibility stands out as a high goal in teaching. The hope is that students will take responsibility for their own learning and behavior. The very fact that they are children, however, means that these students are still learning the value of responsibility and how it applies to life. It isn't fair for a teacher to simply assume a student wants to be responsible—or can be. The teacher's job is to help teach this quality to students.

Rule-following is part of how students exhibit responsibility. Thus the teacher helps facilitate responsibility when reminding children of rules and following up on expectations. Supreme consistency on the part of the teacher will develop this cooperation from students.

Teachers want students to assume responsibility for beginning their own assignments and completing work. They want students to turn in homework, to try learning to the best of their abilities, to keep quiet, and to respect behavior standards in the classroom.

A teacher is an example and can model the *value* of responsibility in a variety of ways. Arriving at school and in the classroom on time is one aspect. Preparing and teaching lessons of quality is another. Patience and control of the class, with dignity, demonstrates responsibility. Not gossiping about students in the faculty room is a factor. Correcting work and returning it in a timely manner shows an example for students. The teacher needs to grade consistently, using previously explained criteria and explaining the grades to students or parents who question the evaluation. Responsible teachers attend school events and parent meetings when appropriate. They attempt to remain objective when discussing student matters. Model teachers telephone parents about student problems or progress. They try to understand the community and environment of their students. They respect and cooperate with administration and coworkers.

Some teachers enjoy making warm puppies out of their students. They set weak expectations for the children. The teacher controls all teaching materials and movement in the room. This forces children to wait for one-on-one teaching for most classwork. These teachers want the children to need them and one can see students hanging close to them, but others may be idle with their hands up and there may be general disruption in the class.

Teachers who teach responsibility have students who walk into the classroom in an orderly manner, sit down, and begin work. There might be a pile of papers in a certain location and each student picks up one as he or she enters the room. Or there may be an assignment on the overhead projector or blackboard. Students see the assignment and get right to work. Very few ask for help at the beginning of these classes.

The warm-puppy teacher, meanwhile, hands out papers at the door and tries to explain something about them to each child. Sometimes nothing is given to the children at the outset of class. That teacher has encouraged students not to begin work until the teacher has explained details.

The responsibility-trained students know they are to have materials and should head their papers with name, date, and class correctly. They may open their books on their own initiative. These students understand that they are free to ask for help, but take pride in trying to work things out independently first. They list homework assignments in a study book or in a section of an organized notebook. Their teacher has taught and reinforced these work habits and recognized and admired this verbally to them.

Teaching responsibility begins the first day of a new class. The teacher explains his or her expectations clearly, keeping them simple. Every day, these points are reinforced in a positive manner. Examples of statements a teacher might make include "Bring three pencils each day, so you have one, if one doesn't work." "Check the Organized Notebook Chart on the bulletin board as soon as you have your notebook organized." "Sign out a pencil or piece of notebook paper, crossing your name off the list when you return it." "Keep a list of books you need for morning classes inside your locker door." Each of these suggestions is an attempt by the teacher to respond to a student's lack of preparedness by helping the student to organize himself or herself more responsibly.

A teacher who did not start emphasizing responsibility the first day can simply consider tomorrow the first day for that class. Students are adjustable and can be told this is a new beginning, to make the class more successful and help each personally in the future. Once the new rules are explained to the students, the teacher must be zealous to help the children follow them.

As important as the positive correction and responsibility guidance for students is sincere praise for their success. "It is great that all of you have your books today. It helps out class get started right away and learn quickly. That will give us time to play your favorite game at the end of this lesson." Comments such as this reinforce positive behavior.

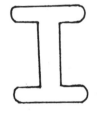

Use "I Messages"

It may seem an insignificant detail to attempt to say *I*, instead of *you*, when directing a child to do something. But it is surprising to note the different responses when one does give *I messages*. This can be a key to success in cooperation from students.

For example, a child has not opened the book to the assigned page, the teacher can direct the child, "You need to open your book now." However, this may produce an unexpected result. The child may simply keep the book closed, reasoning "I don't *need* to open any book. I don't want to open a book." If, instead, the teacher looks directly at the child and says, "I expect the book to be opened," the book will probably be opened. The child is left with no decision about need. The child can simply, without emotion, follow a direction. Other ways to omit the "you" would be to say "All books are to be opened" or "I want to see all books opened." Each example avoids the use of the word *you*, which places the decision in the child's mind.

"You need to get quiet now" is a request that is often ignored by single students or groups of students. Students have a strong desire to be social and will often decide for themselves to continue talking. They don't perceive the necessity for quiet. It is more powerful and successful to say, "I want this class (or Mary) to be quiet now." "I want everyone to hear the film at this time." "I expect this class to stop talking and listen to the lesson." "I need some peace so students can understand this direction." A teacher who sounds convincing (and has this expectation of cooperation) takes charge of the situation.

Class instruction often proceeds more smoothly when the teacher uses many *I messages*. To get the class started, a simple statement such as "I am ready to begin now" can be made firmly. "I am ready to begin the test" is another example. Rarely does a group, or individual student, become stubborn or contrary, because these are unemotional statements that don't really open any door for argument from students.

A child who is upset about a grade, comment, argument with another student, or similar situation does not wish to be told, "You don't need to feel badly about that." The student knows well how he or she feels. Teachers don't need to use *you messages* for consolation. It is more useful to say, "I can see you are upset." "Can I help you?" "I would like to hear how you think this will affect you." "I would like to hear your side of the story."

Developing this technique of using *I messages* requires practice. But teachers get time to practice all day long. It may be helpful to tape-record some lessons to pinpoint situations where change could be made. *I messages* can bring success.

Develop a Calming Voice

Every teacher has his or her own style. It is wise to use that style naturally in one's teaching. However, it may be of help to many teachers to consciously develop and use a calming voice in the classroom. Generally this is a quiet voice which expresses patience and expectation of order and peace in the classroom.

Students may react to a tense or strident voice. It can make them belligerent or uncooperative. Students are highly keyed to the leader of the room. Hundreds of students interviewed have listed "teachers screaming at them" as the factor they dislike most about teachers.

It can be helpful to keep the chin up a little, if tenseness and shrillness creep into the voice. Don't tuck the chin down and project the voice a bit more deeply from the diaphragm. Speak a bit more slowly. Take a *quiet*, calming deep breath.

It is a positive technique to meet students at the door as they enter the classroom. Greet them in this modulated voice, answer questions briefly, and direct them to the beginning task of the day. Stay just outside the door, if this is possible, expecting them to take their seats and begin. Step inside the door to calmly remind a few students (or all, if necessary) that seated, on-task behavior is what you expect. Return to your doorway position, if this is successful, until most students are in.

Then move to the teaching location with the grade book, seating chart, lesson plans, etc. Show calm behavior and expectations that students will stay on task until the teacher is through checking roll, lesson plan, and so on. It may be a long enough quiet time to answer special questions from a student or two or to give out make-up work. Calmly move to a teacher-directed activity if the class starts to become restless. Try to keep the serene climate of the classroom in the teacher's control and practice being calm about it.

If a student is uncooperative, remind him or her that you expect the class to be orderly. Move the student to a seat away from the group, if needed. Use other management techniques to gain this teacher control of serene classroom climate as required. Several of these are suggested in other sections of this book.

The Student Has to Work

The child's job in school is to learn. Teachers and parents do not have to carry full accountability for a child's progress. For example, it is valuable for parents or guardians to read with children, and it is important that a teacher patiently help a child struggle through learning to read, using phonics and word recognition and other techniques for teaching reading. Ultimately, however, it is the child who must work, battle, strain, and put forth real effort to learn skills in reading.

Many methods of teaching multiplication tables or fractions or special math techniques are devised and practiced by teachers, with great sincerity. Teachers need patience to explain and listen to the child, correcting problems in completed work. But there still needs to be the hard-work factor on the part of the child. The child has to strive to learn the presented material. The student's desires and "sweat equity" are necessary factors in learning math.

One could say the same about learning French verbs, the differences between *their, they're*, and *there*, chemistry valences, the order of the planets in the solar system, equivalents in recipe measurements, or many other factors of education. The teacher facilitates the learning, but only the child's necessary input of work, effort, and positive attitude will insure success.

Each child has a certain level of possible achievement. Many times, teachers underestimate this and accept goals too low for the student. Often parents and teachers set goals too high for some children. It is most effective when the child sets his or her own goals for learning. However, if these factors are correctly established, it still is true that the child must *work* to reach to the level of his or her ability.

Teachers don't need to give up when students seem to fall short in effort. Instead, they need to present motivation techniques, expressing high expectations. Positive and honest praise freely given is immensely more effective than any negative techniques, but don't be reluctant to tell students that work is necessary. This is a message to explain to students in an objective manner, modeling the expectations for diligence.

Teachers may want to sharpen methods to stimulate students to desire success and to work hard. Here are some techniques:

1. Encourage the child to set personal goals for learning.
2. Decide and state what level of learning is expected clearly.
3. Take action to get the child on task. (Begin work for the student, move the student to a less distracting location or near teacher's desk, etc.)
4. Notice what methods are succeeding with that student. Change the approach, if the first is not succeeding.
5. Change your approach until the child achieves what he or she and the teacher want. Flexibility gives the teacher power.

Teachers do not have to assume all accountability for learning in a class. Learning is a high responsibility of every student.

Incentives

It can drive a teacher up the wall when some classes will not put away materials and get the room ready for dismissal. Requests and then threats are made. The teacher lengthens cleanup time day after day. Thought is given to simplifying work to eliminate hands-on work and variety in teaching lessons. The teacher becomes discouraged over having to pick up after messy classes. School life gets disorganized and it is difficult to keep track of papers, projects, and materials.

An answer to a problem like this is to use incentives. Assign the students to table groups or row teams to compete against each other. When this system gets working, students can clean up the room in two to three minutes. During these minutes, of course, the teacher *must stay alert* to be aware of which group wins. A welcome reward would be to give each winning group a tiny paper cup of snack crackers. It may be wise to promise the prizes to the group the next day, noting the date and winners on a seating chart or grade book page. This prevents problems of stray reward items in the hallway or in a following class. The following teacher may consider these rewards disruptive. Trail mix, pretzel bits, animal cookies, fish crackers, tiny marshmallows, and dry cereal could be used to fill the cups. Varying the prizes keeps the incentive strong. Consistency of rewards is important when you are first conditioning a new pattern.

Many teachers resist giving rewards or developing systems for incentives, considering them to be bribes and believing that they do not meet a standard of professionalism in education. However, teaching and parenting have always involved incentives for preferred behavior or learning. Many students of today seem to respond best to this teaching technique.

Students in classes everywhere are different. Some students do not require awards and easily accommodate to the behavior or learning proposed by the teacher. It may be that students in any class are on different levels of response to incentives. Some may need extrinsic rewards, such as stickers, pencils, smiley faces, stars, certificates, or candy. Entire classes can be given rewards of cups of orange juice or more time at a favorite activity. This excites these students and makes them strive to succeed. Other students respond best to deserved praise for accomplishment, smiles from the teacher, a pat on the back, posting of exemplary work, and similar incentives. Additional students gain an intrinsic satisfaction of accomplishing their own goals and standards of work.

Teachers can generally assess each class and set an incentive system that meets most students' needs in that class. An early level might be to paste stickers on good work or provide rewards. As the class develops, they may no longer need these extrinsic rewards and will progress to being motivated by deserved praise for accomplishments. The teacher who has more mature students or who has motivated students successfully in steps of incentives may find that internal satisfaction is all most students need as time progresses. There is a sort of continuum of incentive development.

Giving rewards is not simple. Clear criteria for rewards need to be established and explained to students. The teacher has to be consistent and take the time out to give the rewards. They become somewhat of an obligation, since they were promised. Sometimes a secure place to store the rewards, such as stickers or candy, has to be located. It destroys trust to lack the structure of providing the rewards fairly.

The teacher needs to remain calm and to be seen as objective when passing out the rewards. It is wise to use a written list to preclude mistakes. Rewards are not completely positive. It is negative, and a little punishing, *not* to receive a reward. This is why an objective, calm teacher can help model the class behavior at this point.

Teachers also need to evaluate whether the rewards are developing the desired motivational result. Student discussions or evaluations may be beneficial to ascertain this, plus the teacher can usually trust personal judgment. Is the class improving behavior and are students assuming more individual responsibility?

The Five-Wastebasket Answer

Suppose children in a class are being disruptive by walking too often clear across the room to use the wastebasket. What should a teacher do?

The easy answer: get five wastebaskets and place them in strategic spots near the students. This can also help keep the floor clean and aid the children, who need an uncluttered desk to stay on task. It could even prevent having paper flying across the room.

The "five-wastebasket answer" can be used when a teacher expects students to share any item. Providing more scissors, glue, rulers, stencils, dictionaries, etc., may prevent tension and difficulties in sharing. Have enough supplies. If possible, provide racks or cans for scissors, so every pupil has access to one. Each child can be furnished a ruler, dictionary, stencil sheet, glue bottle, or similar small pieces of equipment.

Some schools, or teachers, present lists to parents and guardians of small equipment articles needed by their children at the beginning of the school year or unit of study. If this home supplying is not permitted, budget demands can make it difficult for a teacher to supply enough items for all students. In tight-budget situations, purchasing a few needed articles each year, plus careful monitoring to keep them from being lost, will eventually build a complete inventory. Another possibility may allow a teacher to carefully prepare a list of desirable school supplies and present it to the Parent Teachers' Association for assistance. The teacher who follows up supply requests courteously will eventually build the stockpile the class needs.

It sometimes is more beneficial for students to share. Then the teacher does not want to structure numbers of supplies. Several students can share a set of crayons, or markers, if they are located in a box that can be passed among them. For true cooperative group work, it is usually preferable to have only one paper for illustration, one recorder's log, one research document, etc.

To encourage students discovering and learning together, pairs or three students may be the teacher's choice. This might be preferable when students are learning to use a microscope, sewing machine, or laptop computer, for example. Pairs of sharing students help teach each other concepts and skills with the equipment.

Structuring the use of equipment and supplies is a factor in providing an orderly classroom. Each teacher's situation is different, but the basic planning for success is universal. Misbehavior will diminish and the classroom will be more peaceful if students can proceed to complete projects with readily available supplies.

Hand Up

A noisy or disruptive class can be dealt with in several ways. Many teachers teach a variety of signals for quieting the group. Some use a hand or finger movement. Others use a song or music. Some can simply stare the class into quieter behavior.

One method that can give immediate improvement is for the teacher to simply raise one hand. Students respond to this naturally, often having been taught in Scouts, earlier classes in school, sports teams, or other situations that this means quiet. The teacher may need to wait for a response (usually a bit longer than expected).

It is important for the teacher to state appreciation to the group for getting quiet. "I like the quiet I am hearing." It is essential to immediately lead the group to get on task and take advantage of this response. Simply raise a hand, if they begin getting noisy again.

If the class does not get quiet when the hand is raised, the teacher can say in a clear but calm and somewhat quiet voice, "Everyone who knows you should be quiet, raise your hand." Many will hush. Look directly at any who do not get silent, and repeat, "Everyone who knows you should be quiet, raise your hand." If a few hold out and do not respond, move to that area and repeat your statement. Look sternly at these students. If there are only a few who will not cooperate, simply change these students' seats to a new location in the room. This seat change may result in further disturbance. Calmly raise a hand again. Cooperation should be quicker this time.

The hand signal, plus the teacher direction, is a valuable technique to use when a group is new to you. Examples include an assigned study hall, when unfamiliar students are in this assigned class, or when the teacher has been asked to fill in for another teacher for some reason. These are times when the teacher is often unfamiliar with names or has not built up rapport with these children.

As with most management or discipline methods, success may depend on the poise and appearance of confidence on the part of the teacher. Getting frazzled lets students know you have come undone and don't know what to do. If the teacher expects this hand signal to work, it will carry across to the students and it probably will.

The Broken Record

Many children today do not know what a phonograph record is. They don't know that people listened to their favorite music from records for decades. They would need to be told that records were disks of plastic, with sound tracks cut into them. They might look like a big CD to them. They wouldn't know a 45 from a 33 1/3. One would have to explain to them that a broken record kept playing the same musical phrase over and over again if it seemed useful to explain this teaching technique to your students. Knowing a great deal about music records doesn't matter when using a phrase from this period of time. The technique does work and is effective.

A teacher may find that class cannot begin because some students are not seated. The teacher says, "It is time for all students to be seated." If they do not sit down, the teacher repeats, "It is time for all students to be seated," perhaps a bit more forcefully. The teacher continues to repeat *the same statement* until all sit down, perhaps shortening it a bit to "All be seated." The teacher needs to retain his or her cool and sound objective and unemotional as the statements are presented. The students will usually settle down.

It is important that the teacher resist the temptation to be creative with the instruction. It is *not* a broken record to say, "It is time for all students to be seated." "Sit down." "Take your seats." "Sit in those chairs." This change in wording breaks the repetitive pattern, which would reach the students and change behavior.

For some reason, the students had not chosen to listen to the instruction when it was first given. But the repetition usually reaches them. Perhaps they sit down to avoid the irritation of the "broken record" repetition of the same phrase. For whatever reason, students generally cooperate with the broken record.

An element of the broken record is valuable in teaching, too. Many instructions to students need to be given two or three times. It seems a few are always tuned out the first time a homework assignment is given or instructions are given for a test, for example. Some advanced students dislike hearing the repetition, which they themselves did not need, but certain average and slower students sincerely appreciate their second chance to understand what is expected of them.

Successful teachers put forth instructions and lessons clearly and expect students to comply. Students generally want to cooperate, once they understand.

Corners Are Tight Places

Every teacher has discipline problems. It is necessary to correct the offending child or to change the disrupting behavior. One needs to take careful, thoughtful steps to do this, however. If the teacher acts with quick emotion, it is easy to get the child into a corner. The child in the corner is primed for a fight and it may be impossible to gain his or her cooperation. The term "in the corner" here is meant figuratively. It refers to disciplining a student in front of the group.

A key to corner-prevention is to step into the hallway with the difficult student. Keep the door open and be in sight of the class. The child is a different person away from the peer group. The student will listen more carefully to the teacher here. He or she has no group of students to concentrate on or to impress with tough behavior. The teacher may need to ask for eye contact to gain a real dialogue.

The first priority is for the teacher to state, without emotion, what negative behavior was noted and why it seemed inappropriate. Then, the student should be given a time to respond. An open-ended question might be: "Please explain the disappearance of the pen." Often, the teacher ends up with other students' behaviors to check. If the original situation is the sole problem, it is wise to elicit a promise to improve actions by the student who is being corrected.

Do not meet alone with children, except for this hallway recommendation, in view of the class. Call for help if a child becomes aggressive. Ask a counselor or administrator to sit in on a meeting with a belligerent student.

Other corners teachers create are racially tinged or overly strong words used to a child. Somehow these can never be swallowed back. A teacher can be cruel to a student, too. Pointing out nonachievers, overzealous answerers, those late to task, or messy workers or making similar negative descriptions of students is hurtful. Each of these problems is better handled in a more positive way, one-on-one with the child. Beware of dramatic discipline in front of your class audience.

Kidding can only be done successfully by a small number of persons. It can too easily put the child in a corner. Teasing is a form of bullying—it is fun for the strong one who does the teasing, but it can make the person teased miserable.

An open, calm playing field is the classroom atmosphere desired in teaching. The teacher must remain calm, nonsarcastic, and objective. This keeps students out of hostile corners.

The Active Child

Every teacher has a variety of students in a class. Some of them are especially active. A few of these may even be identified as having ADHD (Attention Deficit Hyperactive Disorder). In addition, most children are naturally active, making it difficult for them to stay seated all day, doing work at a desk or table.

Teachers who understand the need for children to move frequently will structure active periods in lessons during the classroom day. Other teachers have a fear of losing control of a class if the students are allowed out of their seats or when students need to transition to new situations. They try to keep children in their seats, permitting little movement, and their students can become uncomfortable and restless.

The need for movement is a genuine necessity to take into account in lesson planning. Teachers of small children have to plan circle games, recess, exercise periods, and stretch breaks. Older students need action, too. Lessons can be planned for shorter units, scheduling changes of individual tasks to group learning, watching a video, hands-on activities, computer learning, etc. Even a brief period for returning books or papers, finding materials, or clean-up can be a physical break for students.

Individual movement can be permitted as a regular part of classroom behavior. Allowing a student to do routine tasks without asking the teacher first can aid the child who just must move *now*. Students can be allowed to sharpen pencils, throw away paper, go to an area of the classroom for a worksheet or book, use the stapler, or paper punch on a table by the teacher's desk on their own. Teachers who permit this become used to seeing *one* child up and focused on a task need. It may be wise to state limits, such as "No sharpening pencils when someone is talking or reading" or "Only one person out of a seat at a time—everyone can count to one!"

Structuring the movement is the key to avoiding the loss of control with class movement that some teachers fear. One row of students at a time can be invited to return books or papers. Giving small groups different numbers or colors for identification can help the teacher control which groups move at directed times. Numbering and organizing project materials into boxes or baskets can control disruption with hands-on activities. Computer behavior can be taught with a structure of its own; certain students move to assigned computers, where they sit quietly for instructions and follow directions. Preplanning the movements of students can make transitions pleasant.

Some noise is to be expected with activity. The teacher needs to sometimes wait a bit for noise and wiggling to settle down naturally. If this does not happen, a quiet, firm direction for on-task behavior is needed. Hand signals and other discipline techniques may be required. Moving toward an area of undesirable behavior may also be successful to get them quieter. Moving a disruptive child to a time-out area may settle the group. Calm expectation of order is a teacher's strongest ally.

Certain children will demonstrate that they do not understand an assignment by being restless. The teacher can pick up on this quickly and move to that student to find out the problem, helping him or her get on task. If the work is truly too difficult, an alternate assignment may be offered. It is possible to help a child understand an assignment by instructing the child to write down all the new words in it, look them up in a dictionary, and write the definitions. Nonreading students could be asked to copy a portion of the assignments or to draw a feature to illustrate part of the lesson. Sometimes a nonreading student can be paired with a student who will read the assignment out loud. This would need to be done in a quiet corner of the room, as far away from the rest of the group as possible.

Children who finish assignments quickly are often restless. Some of these students need to be encouraged to review and improve their completed work. Teachers with years of experience offer developmental assignments to transfer skills just taught to a new task.

Another answer for the fast child is to have previously taught the class that this is an appropriate time to bring out a paperback book to read for enjoyment. Some teachers have extra-credit vocabulary puzzles or additional work children may locate from a particular place in the classroom. Special computer time could be another prearranged activity.

The ADHD child often needs more space. Seating this child in the front or outside edge of rows may be helpful. One might benefit from a seat near the teacher, for close reassurance. The teacher needs to be watchful to encourage this child to get on task and stay at work. Eye contact, with a smile, may inspire the student. Sometimes a serious stare is needed. A student may respond to being given a soft sponge to drum restless fingers on. Judiciously ignoring some of the nondisturbing actions this child makes may be desirable; for example, the child may drop a book, wiggle in the chair, check in and out of a notebook, etc. Do not hesitate to set boundaries for this child, so the class is not disrupted. It is generally beneficial to discuss behavior problems with the child privately in the hallway or in a classroom office area. Work with guidance counselor, other teachers, administration, and parents to improve serious situations.

Relax and enjoy active children. Learn techniques to control movement and structure activity in the day. The climate of a classroom can be comfortable and orderly.

The Student Team

Some teachers fret over some relationships in classes. These teachers regret placing well-behaved students near troublemakers. Every situation is different and this placement could be unsuccessful. However, it often works well and turns out to benefit both the cooperative student and the difficult child. Students have a strong sense of teaming. High-achieving students often accept the troubled child as a challenge. These positive students often coach the difficult ones on how to succeed and sometimes remind them quickly how to avoid trouble. The high achiever sometimes forms a bond of friendship with this child of misfortune. Students are more likely to feel they are on the same team as the troubled student and do not reject the annoying child as much as a teacher does.

This student teaming is also a factor for teachers to remember as they function as the leader of a class. The teacher is *never on the same team* as the students. Students expect some dignity and distance and leadership from teachers. There are times when everyone in the class, including the teacher, shares class satisfactions, humor, learning, discovery, and enjoyment. However, the teacher is never a buddy or peer of students. Rapport is essential in teaching. It is of high value in reaching students and gives the teacher satisfaction with the job. However, rapport is different from trying to be one of the kids. Students always know this difference.

Teachers who try too hard to be pals may find they lose respect from the children. Students want the teacher to be the authority and are comfortable choosing friends from their own peer group. It's confusing for children to accept direction from the "pal" teacher. Students seek leadership and structure from the adult in charge.

It is interesting that this separation often shows most clearly when a teacher reads a report from a substitute teacher or observes classes with a substitute teacher. The teacher can not believe that their generally cooperative students will give the substitute teacher a hard time, especially when the substitute teacher was trying to be friendly with the children. Many times students will band together to be a disruptive student team. Students seem to relax into some type of team of "us" against the substitute teacher. Students are a team, and teachers are their coaches.

Class Misbehavior

A student throws a small piece of crayon across the class. Soon other students throw crayon bits. The teacher must act quickly to put an end to this class behavior problem. This is time to stop the class and return everyone to their seats, if anyone is up and about the room. Students should be told to close notebooks and books. The teacher can now express displeasure with full attention.

No matter how clearly the teacher explains why this problem makes him or her angry, many children will not understand why this was such a big deal; others simply will not have noticed what was going on. Students dislike it when a teacher scolds the whole class at a time such as this, because most were not participating in the misbehavior.

This is an opportunity for the teacher to pass out a half-sheet of paper (it can even be scrap paper with a clean side). On the board or the overhead projector, the teacher lists four questions and a promise request:

1. Did you throw a crayon piece in this classroom?
2. Did you see anyone throw anything?
3. What dangers to class members are there when objects, such as crayons, are thrown in a classroom?
4. How do you feel about class disruptions such as this in this class?
5. Do you promise never to throw anything in this classroom? If you answer this question yes, sign your name after the yes.

Each of these questions develops understanding of the situation and helps make students buy into the idea that it is a class problem. Those who are perfectly innocent get to tell the teacher so. Others may lie, but they also know they are lying.

The children are not truly requested to squeal on other students with question two, but some may wish to do so. The answers are to be kept private with the teacher. Answers to question four may show the teacher this is a time to discuss dangers and safety, which may help to develop a student emphasis on no disruptions. With the final point, students make a commitment to good behavior. The teacher can keep these papers and show a future disruptive student his or her prior promise. This can be very meaningful, if presented seriously and objectively.

Similar questions can be developed for other classroom misbehavior, at the moment or later. The teacher can create a question list on the computer for an ongoing problem. The teacher could formulate the list after the class, print it, and present copies to each child the following day.

Ten Things to Do

Class is over. The teacher is mulling over a problem that developed during that class. What actions could the teacher have taken to improve the situation? This is a good time to brainstorm possible answers for this predicament. Try to come up with ten solutions. When using this technique at first, write down the ten ideas. As you become more experienced at thinking of multiple solutions, writing them down will be unnecessary.

First, consider the setting of the classroom. Was it too warm or cold? Could that have been prevented or improved in some way? Were the locations of the students appropriate? Do some children need to be separated or do some need to be located nearer the teacher or the blackboard? Does a student need to sit in an area alone or away from the group?

Next, consider the lesson. Were there improvements which could have been made in the lesson being taught when this problem arose? Was it introduced meaningfully? Did it have elements that motivated the students? Was it difficult and was more help needed from the teacher? Is there a way (or more than one way) to cover this material more successfully? Was the teacher enthusiastic about this subject?

Were materials handled successfully? Were there enough books? Were the books clean of offending drawings or words? Are the books reasonably up-to-date? Were there enough markers or scissors or glue bottles or calculators or rulers or other supplies? Did each child have paper and pencil or pen? Was a box or system set up to organize loose equipment? Did the students have desk or table-space enough to complete their work?

Did the teacher handle the situation calmly? (Teachers are human and can lose their tempers, but they must learn to minimize and control this.) Did the teacher move toward the location of the problem? If students were involved in a predicament, did the teacher counsel them separately in the hallway, learning the circumstances? Was there a consequence, if this was appropriate?

Was this an example of a troubled child? Teachers benefit from discussing needs with the student, finding help from guidance or administration, or calling home to gain parents' support. If all has failed so far and if the class structure and safe environment are suffering, a problem child will need to be excluded. Some teachers have a time-out area in the room, a special seat or location for a disruptive student. This would be a first step and keeps the child under the teacher's care. If that does not work, most schools have a time-out policy and provide a supervised location for a student who cannot be successful in the classroom at this time.

When a teacher gets used to listing ten things to do to resolve a predicament, it becomes easier to solve it on the spot at the time of the problem. With experience, a teacher gains a larger repertoire of teaching solutions.

Checklist for Problems

Once a class is over, the teacher may remain concerned about a problem that developed in the class. Brainstorming ten solutions is a helpful technique, but may not work for some teachers, who may prefer to glance through a checklist to accomplish this. The checklist below does not address every type of problem, but may help a teacher quickly evaluate the situation:

1. Could I have waited a bit longer for order to be restored?
2. Could I have been more alert to catch the problem before it got out of hand?
3. Did I introduce this lesson in a way that made it meaningful, so students knew why they were learning it and were motivated to do so?
4. Did I explain clearly what was expected of each student, showing examples and describing a grading scale?
5. Was this an appropriate lesson for this day? Did I consider whether it was the day before a holiday, the day of a dance, party, school-wide achievement test, etc., or the day after a long weekend?
6. Have I been varying my teaching methods? Am I repeating videos, reading assignments, testing, or paperwork too much? Do I illustrate the subject with pictures, videos, music, etc.? Am I varying my teaching style? Do I lecture too much? Do I always assign group work?
7. Would the lesson have been more successful if I had included a hands-on project, such as constructing animals or masks, if studying an African country or an example of a snowflake for science?
8. Is there a student or students in this class about whom I should learn more from guidance, other teachers, school records, or parents or by private conference with the student concerned?
9. Am I building responsibility for behavior in the students, or am I always a controller, directing every movement and word in the class?
10. Am I expecting too much—setting my goals too high? Is this a class with students who need more help or patience?

Five-Minute Vocabulary Game

It is near the end of the class period and the class is a bit restless. This may be a good time to play the "Vocabulary Game." For this, the teacher needs a chalkboard and chalk; simple prizes, such as one sticker or a pencil per winner; and large words posted somewhere in the room. The words can be from a bold, easy-to-read vocabulary list or from posters, signs, or bulletin board titles, etc., that any child can read from his or her seat. Sometimes the teacher also needs the class seating chart to make name identification easier.

The teacher sets the rules: "This is a vocabulary game, using words you can read somewhere in the classroom." (The teacher may want to give additional clues about where the chosen words will be located.) The class needs to be quiet. The child who knows the answer raises a hand. It is a matter of luck, whether a child is called on and whether the teacher is thinking of the same word the child gives as an answer. (Other words would fit the blanks, but it slows down the game too much to stop and ponder this.) The word has to be the one the teacher is thinking to win.

The teacher chooses a word in his or her mind and draws a blank for each letter of that word on the blackboard. Count the letters carefully. Double-check at this time. Then print one key letter (perhaps an *e*) in the correct space. Give a short time for most children to have time to think. Call on a child who has raised his or her hand. If the answer is correct, give out a prize with a smile and positive comment.

If anyone shouts out the correct answer, simply erase the word and go on to another word, reminding the class to stay quiet. Attempt to call on children from each area of the room and girls and boys.

One needs to warn an enthusiastic group, when time is almost up, that the next word listed on the board will be the last word. This allows for an orderly closure to the game and a quiet moment for students to ready their materials for the next class.

The Fight

Hopefully, a teacher will never have to deal with a fight. However, fights can happen in almost any school. Occasionally, the teacher may have been observing a situation grow restless, with loud voices becoming more strident. Other fights may simply begin without knowledge of the teacher. The teacher hears a rumbling in the classroom, looks that direction, and sees two children pummeling each other and the class highly excited. Students may call out, "There's a fight!"

However the fight begins, this is a time for quick reaction from the teacher. The first thing to do is to say immediately, "Stop fighting!" At the same time, the teacher should move *toward* the fight. The order to stop fighting should be repeated again, while approaching the combatants. Try to make eye contact with one and say, "Look at me!" Individual teachers deal differently with the fight at this point, depending on the size of the battlers, the size and strength of the teacher, the training given by the teacher's school system, whether or not other children are pulling the fighters apart, and the personal choice of the teacher.

If the children cannot be separated, the teacher needs to call for help. Many school classrooms have a call button or a telephone. One *responsible* student can be sent to the office or some other *specific* location to get help. Have some responsible students previously selected and noted on the seating chart. The teacher needs to move the other students away from the problem, so they will not get injured. The teacher needs to continue repeating the command to stop fighting. Sometimes a teacher will empty the whole classroom, for the safety of other students, leaving the fighters inside.

During a fight, and after the fight has broken up, a teacher must be careful of how he or she handles each child involved. Expectations of what is proper touching of children can differ, and a teacher may need to learn what is expected and supported by the school system. Very few people criticize touching a child on the upper arm or elbow.

Once the fight has cooled down enough, the teacher can send one combatant to the office, perhaps the calmer of the two, with a pass. This is done to keep them separate until the first child gets to a supervised area. This is sometimes a good time to confer with the remaining student about details, from that child's point of view, of just what happened and why it happened. If at all possible, this is a good time to write some quick notes about what the teacher saw and what this child said while the incident is still fresh. The other child will need to be interviewed later. After enough time has passed (the teacher usually can call the office to check), the other child should also be sent to the office.

If any children were injured, that of course would be dealt with immediately. Help for the injured child needs to be sought right away.

Many fights end quickly, with no child really injured, and the class moves on. The teacher will be expected to write up the situation and perhaps confer with the children and administration about it. It is wise to also telephone the parents of each child and discuss the problem. When talking with parents, it is sometimes recommended to simply say "another child," without naming the other party.

If a teacher has warning signs of a fight, *one* of the belligerents can be sent to the bathroom to cool down. Keep these children separated after the child returns, if at all possible.

It can be quite upsetting, for both the teacher and the class, to have a fight in the classroom. It may be valuable to take time, once all has calmed down, to acknowledge this and then move on to a task at hand. This may be the time to use an emergency lesson previously planned for such difficult times. An example of a calming activity might be to have a box of scripts for a high-interest play at hand. Give one script to each child and ask for volunteers to read each part. Children will generally calm down as they become involved in following the words in a play. It is helpful to plan a few other special activities like this for times of need.

Chapter 4

ℰℭ

Classroom Organization

Teacher's Desk

A teacher's desk can show a great deal about the teacher. In business, some employers base part of their evaluation of their employees on the general appearance of their desks. The top personnel often put a great deal of attention to how each employee's desk looks, sometimes even sending memos suggesting that desks should be more orderly.

Teachers should realize that members of the community, school children, and their school administrators may also make judgments about them based on the appearance of their desk. However, teaching should truly be evaluated by student progress and teaching skill, so some teachers may ignore this "clean desk" subject and concentrate on the intrinsic value of fine teaching.

If maintaining a clear desk is difficult for a teacher who wants things to look better, he or she can resort to several tactics. Some teachers keep a large desk drawer empty and simply sweep off everything into that drawer at the end of the teaching day. Others keep a bookcase to the side of the desk, putting the clutter into or on top of the bookcase.

The teacher's desk should have a drawer full of pencils, staples, rubber bands, and other such supplies. No one peeks into these drawers to judge the order, by the way.

The top of the desk can have a couple of attractive items, along with the roll book, seating chart, and planning notebook. Most teachers want a computer on their desk or at a side table within reach. Keep a clear working space. It may be wise to put the roll book, seating chart, and planning notebook into a drawer at night, if they are not taken home. They are stored a bit more securely that way.

The placement of the desk makes a statement. Some teachers like their desks to face the door, so they can observe entry and exit from the room. They can also note hallway behavior. Some teachers locate the desk at the back of the room, behind children, to observe their seat behavior. Some teachers wish to have their desk in the center front to exert a focus and control of the class. Others want their desk near a window for enjoyment of the view and stress relief.

Certain teachers want the desk to sit like an island, so children have easy, free access to them. Others surround the desk with tables and bookcases to keep their business area a bit private. The subject or grade level has a bearing on placement and surroundings of the desk, too.

The teacher's desk is a rather personal matter, but certain people do make judgments about it. The desk deserves some thought when organizing the classroom.

Flat Spaces

Flat spaces are helpful in a classroom. Every classroom has limitations and many seem too small for much adaptation. However, a teacher can benefit from utilizing flat spaces for teaching needs.

It is useful to include a large table or four small desk tables grouped together in one area of the room. This table area can serve as a natural gathering location for group work, small group-teacher interaction, a time-out spot for disciplining a child, or a larger desktop for a student who needs more space. Some children express a natural wish for more space as part of their learning styles.

Bookcases provide a flat top to display books, pictures, and items of interest to the curriculum. Sometimes there are metal covers on heating/air conditioning units. If these do not get hot or damp and if materials placed there do not interfere with the heating/cooling system, the teacher can use the flat covers in a similar manner. These displays appeal to the visual learning style of large numbers of students. Static visuals, kept up-to-date, do teach the children. Some teachers acquire extra student desks as places to put piles of warm up papers, work handed in, returned work, make-up work, or extra-credit work. They may also use the bookcases for these purposes. Locating some of these materials with free access can improve student's sense of responsibility for their own needs.

One needs to be careful not to overfill a room with furniture. Space creates an atmosphere of peace for children. One needs to balance useful student seating areas and storage areas, leaving enough space for free movement of class members. A creative teacher can arrange the classroom to improve visual education, aid the self-responsibility of students, and provide flexible-purpose areas by including appropriate flat areas in the classroom.

Files and Notebooks

Teachers put hours and hours into preparing lesson plans and lesson materials. Busy days whiz by and paperwork can pile up quickly. The teacher may want to refer to a previous lesson or find make-up work for a child. The instructor may wish to use the lesson or lesson materials again for another class in the future. There are also references, pictures, and examples of children's work that the teacher keeps. In addition, the school gives the teacher directives, reports, schedules, and other written materials.

Organization is essential to keep up with these items, setting up a *simple* system for quick retrieval of these needed materials. It is helpful to have a filing cabinet, but some teachers are satisfied to use portable files that are ready to move to a new classroom next year.

Clearly and neatly label file folders. Create a new file each time there is a new topic. File all the needed papers *immediately*, so these papers don't become a pile to tackle at the end of a tiring teaching day. File some items while children are in the room, if the opportunity is right. *File only what is needed.* Don't stuff files with unnecessary items or more than five copies of anything. Keep files as simple as possible. Initially, arrange everything in alphabetical order. As the files grow, categories, such as school business, poetry, short stories, biographies, staff development, etc., can be organized.

It is helpful to keep copies of daily lesson plans in three-ring notebooks. Begin with a three-inch notebook and organize it with dividers. The dividers can cover time periods, subjects, class levels, etc. The lesson plan notebook can include each day's lesson plans, plus some handout examples used that day.

The key factor in organizing files and notebooks is to put things in them *immediately*. Make this a habit from the beginning of the school year. Keep the notebook on the teacher's desk or right behind it at the ready. Purchase or requisition a strong three-ring punch to use, so you can diligently put lesson handouts into the notebook at the same time the class receives them. In some schools, children treat these expensive punches as toys, so control the use of the punch. Keep files within an arm's length from the desk, so they can be accessed to stow papers immediately. The minute a teacher begins gathering piles of papers to be filed, organization gets lost. Teachers simply do not have much time to file papers. Developing the habit of filing things *promptly* and *limiting* the amount will keep a teacher organized.

Computer files require care also. Take the extra half-minute it takes to properly label and locate items as they are saved in computer files. Think of useful general file folder names and store files in the proper folders. The extra half-minute to save computer files *wisely* will make files easy to locate later.

A possible suggestion in computer filing is to begin each document with the date plus the file topic. Examples would be Nov/01– Grading Policy or Jun/02 – Gettysburg. The first would be filed in the Grading folder. The second would be filed in the Civil War folder. Most computer search programs will locate the key words, and the dates serve two purposes: They help one find most recent or seasonal items, and they are also helpful when one wants to trash old items from the computer.

Save teaching files to floppy disks, CDs, or zip disks regularly. Be faithful about saving to a second source. Then they will not be lost forever if the computer crashes. This also helps one clean items out of the computer memory or hard drive, leaving more space for new items.

Teachers should not have to "re-invent the wheel," rewriting material that has been prepared earlier. Discipline to file materials in an appropriate way promptly will save enormous time and effort and strengthen the teaching program.

Organizing Activity Supplies

Hands-on activities are popular with students and encouraged by proponents of teaching a variety of learning styles. Many students enjoy making things, participating in science experiments, or using math equipment. Some teachers consider manipulative activities disruptive, since children can be careless with them, dropping some, losing some, and even throwing them. Keeping items organized and providing a system of accountability also takes preplanning and some effort. This section discusses class supplies furnished by the teacher, not those children bring for their own use.

If the tools to be used are markers, colored pencils, or crayons, it is valuable to keep group sets in boxes, cans, plastic envelopes, or similar containers. Each container should be marked with a different number. Use a permanent marker to mark each. You will need a set for each group of students. It is also helpful to have two to three extra sets, which can be given immediately to a child who is having a problem with sharing. That child can be moved to a separate location without much class disruption.

A useful item to have when organizing manipulatives is a small wheeling cart. Supplies can be placed on the cart and moved after class to a secure location, if this protection is needed in your particular school. Another simple protective technique is to cover the supply items with a square yard of denim cloth. Students rarely touch or take items which are covered and not in plain view.

It is wise for the teacher to distribute the markers, pencils, or crayons, setting a pattern of giving first row or table group set one, the next set two, etc. This establishes a link of responsibility to the group for their tools. The teacher should briefly check that all needed drawing tools are in each package. If colors are found to be missing or not working, replace them right away. Have a box of spare items stowed away. This ensures that the set maintains value to the children. Students will take better care of supplies that are maintained in top condition. Otherwise they will treat the tools as trash, not replacing the tops or breaking them. If some are missing, the children will borrow from other groups and the accountability control will be lost.

The instructor can request a student from each group to return the tools to the appropriate location when it is clean-up time. Allow enough time for this to be done so you have an opportunity to check each package quickly. If items are missing, this is the time to have the students look for the lost markers, pencils, crayons, or other items. The students need to be held accountable. Focusing on exactly what was returned during the period will lessen the loss of items, because usually the missing items turn up at this point. This is one reason why it is so important to give out full packages in the first place. This avoids any question that the group received a partial set. View the situation objectively. Some items can still be lost, but there will be many fewer with an accountability system. The system may need tightening, perhaps with a sign-out procedure, if too much loss occurs. Each time the children use the supplies, they will remember what is expected of them.

If some of the missing items cannot be located, a teacher can respond to the situation in various ways. Some teachers will express strong displeasure to the class and may limit the offending group's participation in a future project. Others will simply acknowledge the problem and later replace the missing supplies in the package.

Mark math manipulative packages, baskets of colored yarn, glue bottles, plastic envelopes of sequins or feathers, protractors, rulers, scissors, pin cushions of needles, boxes of pins, rolls of tape, and similar student supplies with permanent markers, too. Protractors, scissors, rulers, and similar items can be marked individually. These tools may not suffer as many losses as the art tools. A responsible student can be designated to pass out some of these items to groups. Whenever loss of any supply item becomes a problem, the teacher-directed system for accountability, described earlier, may improve the situation. In certain schools with high losses, some items, such as shears, may need to be chained to a large board or to the work area.

Certain supplies require the teacher to give rules and safety instructions to the students before they are distributed. Some classes, such as science, technology, and family and consumer sciences, have mandated procedures to be followed. Simple rules for using glue would include: "Remember the glue may not wash off, so use only a little, keep scrap paper under your work, and be sure to put the top on carefully before you return it." Rules for safety with scissors, art knives, metal files, chemicals, glass measuring equipment, etc., need to be seriously presented before any child is allowed to touch them. Many children are rarely exposed to tools in their homes, which may surprise the teacher. A pair of scissors can be as dangerous as two knives and each of these sharp items can be considered as a weapon. Students can be asked to demonstrate how to pass these dangerous tools to each other.

The teacher may want to have some old shirts or aprons on hand for children to use for covering their clothing when doing messy projects. Many children can bring these from home to have enough available. It is sad and difficult to deal with spotted and damaged student clothes. Tables can also be covered, using plastic cloth or old sheets. It is wisest to use washable markers and keep the permanent markers under tight control for special use. Misused permanent markers can damage books, children's clothing, classroom furniture, and school walls.

Good organization of student supplies can make hands-on work much more pleasant. Students are far less likely to misbehave with items assigned to them or numbered and counted. It is always valuable for the teacher to state rules and expectations at the beginning of the lesson. A teacher sets a scene for well-behaved classes. The teacher's enthusiasm, expectation for good behavior, and physical closeness by moving about to the working groups, along with a clearly explained project and a supply procedure will create a successful lesson.

If a problem arises, the teacher needs to correct the individual or group immediately. A class-wide problem may necessitate stopping the project, returning the supplies, and giving some general class discipline, such as asking students to write about the problem and securing promises of better future behavior. A child who exhibits dangerous behavior should be excluded from the room immediately, with a follow-up notification of administration and parents.

Hands-on work is an excellent learning method. It can be more like real-life work and develops sequential, creative, and thinking skills. Preplanning and organization can make it enjoyable for both teacher and students.

 ## New Books

When new books arrive in a classroom, it prevents many future problems if they are prepared for student use before being made available to the children. An experienced teacher knows that it can be difficult to get new books again and these books may need to be used for many years. New books deserve special care. School systems vary widely and some simply provide up-to-date books as an expected standard. In other systems, however, teachers must wait years and years for new books and are very anxious to replace the tattered ones they have been using.

The following suggestions are for classroom sets of books that stay in the classroom. This is not necessarily the way children should care for the individual books that are checked out to them to take home for the unit or class year. Some of the following recommendations may not be necessary in all schools. These suggestions are intended to help the teacher who is in a school in which the students are careless with books. Some children don't have a view of long-term use of books and are hard on them. Others simply don't like books and want to damage them. Some think it amusing to mark them with offensive words and pictures. Some simply want to "leave their mark" on the books by writing names or initials or making drawings in them. Carelessly handled books are inevitably damaged and students value these books less if they are in poor shape.

Several procedures can help minimize some of these problems, provided they are implemented before the books are passed out. If it is not done automatically by the school, most teachers will mark each book inside its cover to show that it belongs to the school. It is wise to number every copy in an easy-to-see location, as well. The teacher should count and check the number of books in a regular manner. It may be best to pass them out individually if students in a particular class are prone to damaging books. In that way, numbered books can be associated with individual children and the teacher can gain accountability for who handles each book. Books in use should be checked often enough to know their quality and spot damage. Students generally help with this by telling the teacher if a book has a marked or torn page. Emphasis on the care of books, and the fact that a student knows the teacher can easily discover that he or she damaged the book, may lessen problems.

As with most problem areas in teaching, some preparatory teaching can lessen the book damage problem. Student cooperation will probably result if the teacher takes a few minutes before passing the books out to point out to the class how nice it is to have clean, fresh books. Students can be asked to help in keeping them that way, and they probably will. Students generally follow positive ideas presented by a teacher, and many help support the clean book practice by reminding other students. Cooperative students in a loyal class often instill lots of discipline for the teacher with their support.

Students can assist in preparing brand new books for use by opening them in a careful manner, which will protect the binding and future openings of the book. Students should lay the books on the spine and open them a few pages from the beginning and a few pages from the end. Then the pages should be pressed down with a finger near the spine at each end of the book. This process is repeated, opening a few pages more from each end and pressing them down until the middle is reached. If this is carefully done, the book will now open easily and will give longer wear.

Returning the books requires a system that ensures that all the books are picked up and stored in an orderly manner. It is helpful to have special shelves or a bookcart for storing the books. One student can be assigned to the book storage location to count the books as they come in. Another method would be to have a row or group leader who is responsible for seeing that his or her row has turned in the books. Numbers that relate to the rows or groups could be helpful, if book loss is a problem in a certain class. Generally it is sufficient that a teacher simply observe the return of the books. A distracted teacher, accomplishing a different task at this time, may find out that books are lost.

Many school systems have directed plans for dealing with new books and with book collections at the end of the period of use. These can involve using a special stamp, inventory forms, vouchers students sign for lost or damaged books, etc. It is wise to follow these directives, adding the suggestions given above to keep the books in good shape. It is an element of respect toward students for the teacher to work to keep attractive and appealing books for their use.

Chapter 5

℘℘℘

Personal Needs

Believe in Yourself

 It can seem that the "grass is always greener" in the classroom across the way. The students appear to be well behaved in that room. One observes some teachers who seem to discipline children with ease. Students seem naturally respectful for certain teachers.

Any teacher, and particularly a new teacher, can feel discouraged at times when things do not go perfectly in his or her class. Young teachers believe that if they were older, things would go better. Older teachers are sure that younger teachers have more energy for the job. Teachers in the middle have enormous responsibilities for their own children or for their aging parents, and are sure teaching is easier for younger and older teachers.

The truth is that all types of teachers are beneficial to children. Adjusting to different teachers' styles prepares children for relationships in the world of today and in their futures. *Believe in yourself.* Each teacher has unique qualities to bring to teaching and there are eighty-five good ways to teach. There may be 85,000 good ways.

You will benefit from following recommended school practices; introducing structure, consistency, positive messages, and preplanning in your classes, and having a sincere liking for children. After this, your own personality and style deserve to be given credence. Trust your good instincts and practice self-esteem building. Credit the long years of preparation to know the subject and the curriculum. Realize that the chosen degree of firmness needs to be comfortable in order to be successful.

To thine own self be true. If you are a friendly person who likes children, don't be afraid to show it. Allow the children to relax, within appropriate structure and rules, so teaching and learning are enjoyable. Another teacher, who likes order and quiet, can reinforce these principles within the class. A teacher is like someone playing a card game; however, each teacher is dealt from a different deck of cards and plays the game with a different strategy. Children adjust to the styles of all their teachers. They quickly size up what is expected of them in each class and generally go along with the teacher's plan. The teacher needs to remain confident that his or her techniques will work. It is that air of competence that one is secure within oneself that shows.

Teaching is a constantly evolving job. One is always modifying for changes in children and the educational program. You may observe a technique another teacher succeeds with. Try it to see whether it works for you. Take classes and workshops to build teaching skills and bolster self-confidence. Keep developing the assurance that you are an excellent teacher and have a special contribution to make to education.

Dress for Success

Most people have heard the phrase "dress for success" and usually relate it to businessmen and women who are trying to get ahead. How a teacher dresses can affect student respect and behavior and the way the teacher is viewed by other faculty, supervisors, parents, and people in the community, too. Carefully chosen clothes may increase others' regard for the teacher.

Back in the 1950s, even kindergarten teachers wore spike heels or a suit and tie. That was a restrictive way to dress, and most of us are happy that today's standards are more relaxed. However, "dressing for success" still promotes prestige and respect today. On the first day of a new class, a teacher can immediately command more respectful discipline from a class by wearing a dark suit or dress to project a businesslike visual image. Later in the year, teachers' bright colors seem to be appealing to students, especially elementary school students.

Students are particularly sensitive to what teachers wear. They are at an age where they study fashions of dress—on each other and on music, TV, and movie stars. Likewise, they look extra hard at every detail of a teacher's mode of dress. They will forgive almost anything, which is what certain sloppy and dowdy teachers count on. They will also enjoy stylish—though not faddish or silly—dress from their teachers who express respect for the job of teaching and for the students as worthy persons to dress well for.

The kindergarten teacher of today is better off in pants and comfortable shoes, to be able to crouch, bend, sit, and move with the active child's activity. This comfortable dress for activity is also appropriate for most elementary teachers.

High school teachers are a most independent group. It is an affront to many of them to even read about something as personal as how to dress. One hears, "I am only interested in teaching theorems of geometry." Obviously, teaching skills, knowledge, and thinking are of prime importance. However, high school students are only a few years, or months away from the world of work. It benefits them to have mentors, teachers, and role models who dress in a businesslike manner.

Parents and community members are sometimes shocked when they come into a school and say, "I couldn't tell the teachers from the children—everyone was dressed in jeans and sweatshirts." Jeans are probably the most practical, attractive, and useful item of clothing ever devised. Some jeans, though, when they are soiled or ragged or fit badly look absolutely horrible. There are teachers who should not wear jeans at school, except for sports or relaxation in nonwork times. A teacher must look into a mirror critically and decide what decision to make about wearing jeans.

New teachers often find their wardrobes are limited for their first years of teaching. Many times, familiar college clothes can be dressed up with a blazer, vest, dressy sweater, or scarf. Select these items carefully, perhaps in neutral colors that go with everything else in the wardrobe.

In observing thousands of teachers over three decades, I have observed that teachers who dressed "up" a bit more than the crowd eventually became the leaders of the school system. These were the ones noticed for selection as principals, assistant superintendents, or supervisors. Of course, some teachers remained happy as clams, still teaching geometry theorems all their careers—it is not for everyone to "advance." But it is helpful for each teacher to feel respected and successful. Dressing with thoughtfulness may achieve that.

Stress

Stress can be a serious problem in schools. Students surveyed in recent years have listed stress as their biggest problem, above AIDS, teen pregnancy, drugs, and similar fears. It may be that stress includes fear of these health issues as well as schoolwork, tests, homework, parent expectations, social pressures, and other problems for them.

Teachers also say that stress is a large concern for them. Some people who leave teaching cite stress as a major factor. If you walk about a school and observe staff in typical classroom situations, you may see certain classrooms that appear to be functioning with a good deal of tension. You see restless students, many not on task. Some children are simply chatting with a nearby student. Others are slumped in their seats, with an "attitude." There is a din of noise in the classroom. The teacher does not have the students' attention but is trying to gain it. This is not rowdy misbehavior, but this classroom is stressful for the teacher and those students who don't like noise and disruption.

Visiting other classrooms, however, you could hear a pin drop. The teacher is directing all activities and students don't dare to move or say a thing. Both the teacher and the students appear tense. This is another view of stress in the classroom. This teacher has inflexible expectations and often gets very tired with the constant vigilance this requires.

There is a middle ground a teacher can set to lower stress. In fact, lessening stress can be built into the climate for a classroom and planned for in lessons and classroom management.

Meeting students at the door with a friendly greeting is a good beginning. Students can be expected to take their own seats and begin the warm-up assignment. This "start work right away" procedure needs to be established by the teacher as a regular routine, which is expected by the students. The teacher may inform the class of the beginning task the day before or provide a regular notebook assignment, a board assignment, or a special worksheet that the students are handed at the door or can find in a special location in the room. Students are expected to work on this task while the teacher is at the doorway.

When it is time to actually start class, the teacher can then structure a loose opening. Students can be expected to continue with the simple task, begun while the teacher was in the doorway, allowing the teacher to take roll, visit with a couple students who have questions, etc. As students learn this regular procedure, a great deal of tension is eliminated.

To introduce the day's lesson, the teacher can move closer to the students. This location can be varied, from the front of the room to sides, and so forth. Moving too much makes the students a bit nervous, but a change or two can focus attention. Teachers who smile a lot, relax most children. Looking right at the students can aid in holding their attention, too.

Teachers can practice developing a calm, low voice. This, of course, is a very personal suggestion and will not interest or work for some teachers. In surveying hundreds of students, however, it was clear that one of their great dislikes in school was having teachers scream at them. Harsh, stringent, hostile, frustrated voices do not calm students. Speaking in a calm, almost quiet voice can be very peaceful for them. The teacher needs to be sure to speak clearly and loudly enough for the farthest child to hear. By looking at that child occasionally, one naturally should speak loudly enough.

It is wise not to confront students, to keep the peaceful class-room. Most students with react with hostility if backed into a corner. For example, don't say, "You have to read that paragraph now." Sometimes, the child simply will not read at that time. It can be a simple reason, such as a sore throat. Speak to the child later to find out why he or she was reluctant and, unless it is a valid reason, do call on that child again in the future. Simply put, do not fight it out in the classroom.

Don't plan too much lesson material for the time available. Simplify or shorten the lesson, if it starts to make everyone tense about finishing in the time allowed. It is also wise to provide a long enough time for clean-up. If the class is not finishing in the allowed time, lengthen the clean-up period by two to five minutes. If that does not work, think of a reward or incentive system to eliminate that problem. A great deal of stress is avoided if teachers plan effectively to finish the class on time.

Recommended ways for a teacher to lower personal stress include breathing deeply from the diaphragm, or posting a favorite picture of a beach or mountain or puppy on the classroom wall to look at during stressful moments, to gain some pleasure and relaxation. Changing activities may result in a calmer group. If needed, management skills such as hand signals may be used. Practicing ways to structure a calm classroom can create less stress and add enjoyment to teaching days.

Teachers can minimize stress by relaxing over lunch, using as much of the short time to simply sit and eat, not correcting papers or running off worksheets. Choose a place to eat where conversation will be amusing or positive. Another choice would be to eat in the classroom, with music or a good friend to chat with. Leave school early enough to allow time for enjoying life. Assign a time goal for leaving school each day. Walking and swimming are particularly good stress reducers, as is most exercise. Consciously working to reduce stress aids a teacher in doing a better job with students.

Saving Energy

Fatigue at the end of a teaching day is a common problem. Conserving energy, to prevent this afternoon exhaustion, deserves a thoughtful plan and some self-discipline. The ideal would be to work eight- to nine-hour days and use the rest of the day to live life.

This requires discipline, because it means the teacher needs to begin working immediately when he or she arrives at school, throughout one's planning period, and once the children leave in the afternoon, to complete the eight- or nine-hour day at school. These are the three blocks of time to plan lessons, correct papers, record grades in the computer or grade book, check with guidance or administration or co-workers, etc. Teachers, who really *use* these blocks of time can get most of these tasks done.

However, it frankly is difficult for an English teacher with an enormous paper-correcting load or for a science or family and consumer science teacher who has to set up lab materials to get everything done in this time frame. The computer teacher may require more time to set up or troubleshoot hardware. A large number of school conferences and meetings may also shorten the time available to accomplish work. Be careful, though, not to make excuses for all teaching loads. Discipline at using the time afforded at school can minimize the need for carrying work home. To save energy for an energy-demanding job, one needs to endeavor to get most work done at school in a reasonable amount of time.

A teacher should preserve a proper lunch break. (How one wishes it was a lunch hour!) Lunch is not a time for paperwork or business conferences, except in an emergency. The food chosen is a great factor in providing energy. The famous Nutrition Food Triangle Balanced Diet does perk up a person. This diet includes a protein, such as meat, eggs, peanut butter, or cheese. Each meal should also include a vegetable or fruit. Some carbohydrates, such as bread or pasta, is another main component. Milk or yogurt is the fourth element. Be careful about eating large quantities, fried foods, or rich sweets if *pep* is desired after lunch.

Many teachers drink lots of coffee, tea, or colas. The caffeine is pleasant for a quick spike of alertness, but watch to see whether a real drop of energy in the afternoon follows. Moderation of caffeine may be better.

Active teachers do not get many opportunities to sit down. It can be valuable to have a tall stool that one can easily move to the doorway or to an area of the classroom. The instructor can sometimes perch on the stool when greeting children entering the classroom or when giving a test. Sitting at appropriate times during the day does conserve energy.

Certain advertisements for shoes stress that they are comfortable for teachers, who are on their feet so much. This points out that choosing comfortable shoes is important. Shoes may deserve to be the most expensive part of one's wardrobe.

Developing a calm, firm manner with children can also prevent teacher fatigue. Instructors who are always fussing at the children tire quickly. The teacher who *calmly* and *consistently* develops the discipline structure in the classroom has a cooperative, peaceful class and expends less stress energy.

Certain difficult students sap energy from a teacher. One needs to zealously work to develop rapport with these students, not letting the situations escalate. Do not be afraid to ask for help, if it is needed. Continue to ask for help until there is a resolution to the problem. Don't grin and bear problems—work to solve them.

Remember the energy factor when planning a day's lesson. Limit the paperwork assigned that will have to be corrected later. Plan complicated labs and projects for the beginning of a week when energy is high. Plan quiet activities on Friday afternoons, when the children and the teacher are more tired. *Do* plan all the activities to be learning based and relevant, of course.

A teacher needs a regular exercise program. Talk with any teacher who swims, plays tennis, runs, lifts weights, does aerobics, or plays basketball or volleyball. They will usually report that the exercise feeds their energy and sense of well-being.

The suggestion to get enough sleep sounds like a personal and intrusive suggestion. But most of those peppy and active children in classes have been nagged to get plenty of sleep, and teachers need enough sleep to keep up with them.

Preserving energy is a big factor for successful teaching. It deserves serious thought and attention and brings real personal rewards.

A Locked Private Area

Experienced teachers have heard numerous times about staff members who have lost money, a purse, or something else dear to them. Every staff member needs a secure place to keep some private items. Some schools provide lockers, locked closets, or locking desk drawers. It takes self-discipline to always put special personal items in these locations, but it is wise to make this habit.

Teachers usually enjoy children, almost considering some classes like family. They don't want to lock things up because they want to trust the students. Most students can indeed be responsible, and for them, this locking is not needed. However, it is not unusual for a child to take a purse or money or a special picture that is cherished by the teacher. The student may need or want money badly, may be a habitual thief, or may simply be affectionate toward that teacher, wanting so have something that belongs to the teacher. Some students have expressed the idea that anyone who leaves something where it can be stolen is a sucker and deserves to lose it. Certain students consider taking items to be a sport, enjoying the sense of danger and getting away with the wrongdoing.

Some teachers who have lost items are devastated. Most at least feel high disappointment at the outrage. It is personally hurtful to have this loss from persons one is so close to as members of one's class or school. Some teaching enthusiasm can be diminished. In addition, losses of a wallet or purse can mean lengthy calls and trips to replace cards, licenses, etc. Theft is a serious problem.

Most school systems and administrations take theft seriously. They will endeavor to retrieve the lost items, and often do. This requires a great deal of effort and cooperation. Sometimes, however, there is no return of the lost items. Either way, there will be a number of people who wish the teacher had locked the personal property up in the first place.

Occasionally, it will work for the teacher to explain the loss and request help from the class for its return. It is helpful if an administrator can work with the group before the students have moved to another location. It can be helpful to know which students have left the room for the bathroom or elsewhere. Sometimes children can be requested to name, on a piece of paper, the person they think may have taken the item, without signing their names to identify themselves. In some cases, a student will privately tell the teacher who took the property.

Locking valuables up can be an important element of continuing to enjoy teaching and children. A responsible teacher will suffer fewer disappointments.

Correcting Papers

Watch teachers carrying heavy bags to and from school. These totes are generally full of student papers to correct at home. Some teachers also correct papers at meetings, in the hallway, or when riding in a car to a party or vacation location. Correcting assignments is a time-consuming part of a teacher's life.

Some teachers simply assign paperwork freely—never intending to correct much of it. That practice is the prerogative of that teacher, but students soon become aware of it and deal with the assignment policy in varying ways. It can be fairer to students for the teacher to make a plan for paperwork expected from students and to clearly explain how the assignments will be evaluated. The number of students a teacher deals with is a factor to consider when making the plan. The large classes many teachers have make paper correcting even more tedious.

A teacher can limit the correcting task in one of several ways. One way is to assign less paperwork. You may be tempted to quiet the class by saying "Outline three pages," "Write a summary," or "Read chapter four and answer questions about it"—but stop to consider the hours the assignment will take to correct. Perhaps students could be selected to give oral summaries of an assignment instead, thereby eliminating hours of correcting. Think several times before assigning unneeded paperwork.

When a written assignment *is* assigned, explain how it will be graded. Ideally, the teacher should read all students' answers, giving credit for achieving the clearly explained grade factors or rubric standards. If the teacher corrects spelling, punctuation, and grammar as well, the student has a chance to see where improvement is needed. Some teachers believe they never have time to do this. Others circle student errors and demand the children make these corrections and return the papers.

An assignment that took considerable effort from the student merits a comment as well as a grade. Positive statements, such as "excellent," "outstanding," and "terrific," are good, but it is more valuable for the teacher to give comments, like "The character development was well done in your story," "This electric bell diagram is correctly and clearly completed," or "I enjoyed reading about your stirring experience at Gettysburg."

It does help to correct a few papers in the hallway or at convenient moments during the day. That makes the pile lighter. Don't allow your mind to wander too far from the hallway supervision or study hall monitoring job at hand, though. Also, it is often considered rude to correct papers while attending a meeting.

It is important to stay abreast of paper correcting. If one lets too many assignments pile up, the job may never get completed. That is unfair to students. A heavy load of papers from substitute teachers can be especially daunting. It would be wise to structure substitute assignments with less accumulation of paper.

Some teachers have students correct their own work and some instructors can carefully have students correct each other's work. Some people consider this an invasion of a child's right to privacy. Correcting a student's written work is a clear way for a teacher to understand the student and his or her understanding of the topic. Correcting student work is an extremely important part of teaching.

The teacher who utilizes before-school time, planning time, and after-school time will bring fewer papers home. Some teachers manage to get all their paper-correcting done at school, but that requires self-discipline. It pays to give careful consideration to the creation of student assignments and to the realistic completion of correcting them.

Chapter 6

✂️

Professional Relationships

Parent Conferences

Teachers want to communicate well with parents. The goal of helping a child to succeed in school and life is shared by parents and teachers. Cooperation and support for each other and the child should be the goal of parent conferences.

Some parent conferences are informal and unplanned: a chance meeting at the mall, for example. These are valuable moments to initiate a relationship. It is useful to introduce yourself and say something positive to demonstrate your pleasure in working with the child. It could be a time to note that you would like to schedule a meeting with the parent, if there is a situation to discuss.

Another informal conference could happen when a parent brings a child to class or picks the student up. These are generally best kept for friendly greetings, with few open discussions about the child in front of other children or even the child involved. Some teachers may try to locate a private place for more conversation, but otherwise it would be wise to schedule a formal conference for more discussion.

Back-to-school nights usually are planned to allow parents and teachers to meet each other and for teachers to present information such as curriculum and grading policy. Again, these conferences are times of little privacy and are mainly a group experience. Teachers may find they can share brief personal information with parents, but should suggest scheduled conference times to share a problem with a child's parents. It can also be uncomfortable to praise certain students in this group setting. Other parents, overhearing this, will feel their child is being left out. If the teacher talks too long with some parents, others will be resentful. The teacher can write down the names and phone numbers of parents who want to communicate more, and later ask the office to schedule personal conferences.

Regularly scheduled conferences, for most children, can be an excellent way to establish rapport for working together with parents. It is important for all to have a comfortable sitting area. A decision needs to be made as to whether the child should be present. The teacher should begin every conference by sharing something pleasant about this child, presented in a smiling and sincere manner. It is important to keep the conference positive. When there are points for improvement to be discussed, it is essential that the teacher present them in an objective, nonemotional manner. "Katrina is a wiggly worm," "She is always a restless, difficult, child," and "She drives me up the wall" are examples of poor, emotional communication. "Katrina is an active child, gets out of her seat at inappropriate times, and distracts the class" would be a more positive comment that could help the conference move to understanding. Katrina's parent is more likely to agree with the second presentation and admit that the problem exists at home, too. When teacher and parent share the problem, it is easier to work together for improvement and support.

Once the situation is understood clearly, it is important to work toward a solution. Simply having the parent or parents on the same team, with goals for improvement, can go a long way toward improvement. Some parents may offer some restrictions at home to correct the problem or can offer a suggestion that has helped in the past. The teacher may share ideas he or she plans to use, such as changing the child's seat, offering an incentive or restriction, changing part of the child's curriculum, referring the child to a guidance counselor or to someone in administration, etc. It is wise to conclude with a stated goal to improve the situation. Again, in conclusion remember to say something positive about the child and this opportunity to meet together.

A few parent conferences can be highly charged. Some parents have a reputation for being argumentative. The teacher may previously have had a difficult time with the parent. There may be a serious disciplinary problem to discuss, such as theft or serious harassment or abuse of other students. If a teacher senses the conference could be awkward, it is wise to ask an administrative or guidance person to be present. This third party can be valuable in keeping the conference on track, in many cases preventing high emotions from erupting. In addition, there is a witness and the teacher is not left with his or her word against the parent's about what was said at the conference.

A parent can sometimes come to a conference in a belligerent or aggressive mood. It's wise not to urge the parent to "calm down." The teacher can recognize the parent's anger in an unemotional manner and listen. It may be that the teacher will want to call in an administrator to share a conference that has become difficult. It may be valuable for the teacher to write down some points the parent makes, even reading them back to show understanding. If the hostility does not end, one can say, "Thank you for sharing feelings," stand up to conclude the meeting, and try to reschedule another conference for another date. "Thank you" is a particularly helpful phrase in many hostile situations.

Occasionally, a parent may want to record a conference. In most school systems and states, the teacher has the right to refuse the recording. Another sensitive point could be the grade book. In most cases, the teacher has the right not to show the grade book to the parent. Other children's grades are in this book and they deserve the right to privacy. It may be best to list the child's grades on a sheet of paper that may be given to the parent.

It is essential to present a calm, in-charge image, being exceptionally careful not to say any words that will be regretted in the future. Some people are taught to smile and say, "Thank you for your information or your opinion," but not to respond to hostile statements with argument. Stay confident that you are the teacher and in charge, and if necessary, stand up and state there is no more time to close off a conference that is not going well.

Most parents are pleasant people and meetings with them are enjoyable. Experienced teachers understand the value of parents. They send the school their best hopes in their children. Be accepting and appreciative of parent interest and concern. Almost all of them love their children, and children love their parents, even difficult parents. Parent conferences are a valuable tool for success in working with students. The teacher who shares the goals for children with parents puts education in a stronger position. Eventually many teachers work with the same parents for several siblings and can relate to families in their school community.

Upset with Grades

"Why did I get this grade?" "Why did my child get this grade?" "Why are so many of your students getting low grades?" These are three questions that trouble teachers. Some teachers become very defensive when they hear any of them. It is helpful to deal objectively when answering them, controlling emotions and dealing directly with each question. Teachers need to prepare from the first day of class to answer these questions.

It is essential for the teacher to set up a grading policy from the start that will help answer questions about grading. This subject is covered earlier in this book. A copy of the grading policy can be given to each student or it may be posted in the classroom. It is a teacher's responsibility to follow the policy, setting up a grade book or record to reflect this. The grading policy should be explained clearly to the students and to the parents. It is important to repeat grading guidelines regularly to the students, too. Young students need reminders.

A procedure should be established for making up work for times that a child misses school. A goal would be to have getting make-up work be the child's responsibility, but this does not work for all children, especially younger ones. Students do not always understand the concept that work was completed by the class while they were gone. Nor do they comprehend that they are accountable for this missed work. The teacher must select the make-up work and explain it to the child, and reminders are generally necessary. The policy about what happens when make-up work is not turned in needs to be explicit and understood by all.

At any time during the grading period, a child may ask to see his or her progress. A patient teacher will take the time to explain the child's grades. Some teachers require students to keep a running list of their class grades in their notebooks.

For some reason, many children remain naïve about grades. If they have three papers with high grades, they assume they have a high grade. Students may not count their low grades or missing assignments. These children do not grasp the concept of averaging grades.

Teachers need to explain to the class how grades are averaged. They can also remind students whose grades are weak that their grades need improvement. Many school systems require teachers to inform students and parents of the grade status at the middle of the grading period. In this way, there is still opportunity for the child to improve. The teacher can provide opportunities to make up missed work or methods to improve grades.

Having clear grading policies will lessen the questions at grading time. It can also be helpful to inform students what their grades may be a few days before mid-term progress reports and before final grades are turned in. This diffuses questions at the end. It allows a child to ask the teacher how to improve the grade before notice is actually posted. Improving the grade may or may not be possible. If not, the child has an opportunity to adjust to the grade status and may prepare his or her parents.

When answering questions about grading after they are presented, be clear and objective. Be prepared to back up the grade with the grading policy and grade record. It is not appropriate to show a student, or a parent, other students' grades, however. A secure teacher will usually stick by a fair and valid grade and will not change the grade. That decision is personal and would be made on an individual case-by-case basis. Mistakes can be made.

When a parent complains about a grade, try to schedule a conference with an administrator or a counselor present. It is important to preclude having an emotional confrontation with a parent. Confrontation is more likely, if the meeting is a two-person parent-versus-teacher setting. Some schools now hold all parent conferences in the gymnasium or cafeteria so other teachers and administrators can be present.

Give the parent and third party, if present, a comfortable place to sit. Begin and end the conference with a positive statement about the child, if possible. A helpful way to deal with strong critical comments is to say, "Thank you for sharing your concerns." Listen carefully. It may be helpful to repeat back some of the points to assure the parent that you are hearing them. An example would be: "You believe your child completed all assigned make-up work." Then explain what the grade record book shows for each point. Calmly and objectively explain the grading standards and how that child met them.

If a parent becomes angry or abusive towards the teacher, the teacher or administrator should stand and end the conference. A future conference can be scheduled, if necessary.

In a compatible conference, it is wise to focus on how both the parent and teacher can help the child's improvement. Clearly explain how the child can better meet expectations. Generally, it can be helpful for the parent to check the child's agenda or study record book or notebook each evening. A daily progress report form may be initiated; the guidance office often provides these. The child brings the sheet to each class and teachers note daily comments for the parents to monitor progress. At many schools, a parent can check the Internet Web site of the school or the teacher. This may list homework for a child's class and tell what the class is doing. The teacher should thank the parents for their support and taking the time to attend the conference when the meeting is over.

If a principal questions a teacher's grades, a teacher may feel threatened or upset. It is helpful to recognize, without emotion, that this is the principal's job. It is wise to set up an appointment with the principal to objectively discuss the situation. Be prepared to clearly explain the grading policy and grading record. The teacher may believe a group of students is simply not up to meeting standards. If the principal has a valid question about the grades, it is wise to study the grading policy and grade record again. Too many low grades may signal a need to improve teaching technique, pacing of lessons, repetition, clarifying instructions and expectations, or any number of teaching factors. Some school-wide factors or student motivation factors may also be making it difficult to get students to meet standards. Teachers should endeavor to meet challenges, be open to change, hold high expectations for the students, and aim toward students' success.

Co-workers

Choose to spend time with co-workers who are positive and help you feel calm without stress. A school has principals, custodians, cafeteria workers, other teachers, secretaries, a media specialist, a nurse, guidance counselors, bus drivers, security personnel, and other staff members. All of these workers are essential to the school and it benefits a teacher to build relationships with each group. But give most time to those who contribute to one's sense of well being.

Deal sensitively with those staff members who are difficult to get along with. Clearly communicate needs and business. Choose words carefully by *stopping to think* before saying something that might cause conflict. You can either say nothing, if a subject will be a problem, or simply state the situation objectively. Take care not to be emotional. Do not be afraid to be assertive to explain your needs. Intimidation from another staff member should not deter your goals. Be carefully polite in dealings with difficult co-workers. It can be helpful to try to develop rapport by sharing other interests. If that does not work, do not spend more time than is necessary to complete business with them.

Considerate relations with custodians can be beneficial. You are likely to be richly rewarded with help from them when it is needed. The teacher needs to be sensitive and not constantly fuss for assistance. Be aware of the many people directing and calling for these workers. This is why patiently waiting for aid is necessary. Don't forget to thank these helpers.

Keep a friendly, professional relationship with principals and other administrators. Be creative, if necessary, to get along, because these relationships are personally essential. Don't use up too much of an administrator's time, but don't be afraid to ask for help. Try to follow suggestions given if there is a problem, and then ask for aid again if help is still needed. When an administrator requests a special report or task from you, try to put top priority into getting the task done promptly.

Guidance personnel can be of real help for your problems with difficult children. A teacher has many resources to get help, but this is an excellent one. It is courteous to arrange for a convenient time to confer with the counselor about a problem child. It is wise to read the child's guidance record before the conference. Objectively state the problem and see whether it can be worked out. In an emergency situation, of course, the teacher should attempt to confer with a counselor right away. Don't hang back for the appropriate time if it is that urgent.

Many schools have recently added security personnel, who can aid teachers. Work with them to support good hall behavior. These staff members may be able to share some insights about students with the teacher, because they often build relationships with some of the most troubled children.

A teacher will find fellow teachers can be a great source of information and assistance. Schools often sponsor mentor teachers to aid new teachers who need help. This can be an excellent source of assistance, especially if the mentor has a shorter teaching load to provide time for observations and sharing. These mentoring situations need communication time to work. A full day of teaching affords little time for teacher training.

Informally, a teacher benefits immensely by discussing education with other teachers. Choose those who are positive and can be helpful. Try the ideas and methods suggested, but do not assume they are better than your own. Concepts are good only if they work for you. It is not stealing to use ideas from others—this is the way the teaching craft has been passed on for centuries. Sometimes other teachers can suggest plans that help with behavior of specific students, too. Use all the ideas you can get. Discovery and change are essential in education.

Do not get in the habit of discussing how difficult teaching is, how impossible some children are to work with, how soon one can retire, or similar negative concepts. Seek out positive co-workers instead, when possible, to keep on track. Work at building teaching skills and successes and enjoy the challenges of the job.

Observations

Teachers often feel fear or discomfort when supervisors observe and judge them. However, evaluation of teaching in a classroom is essential to establish standards and goals for the teacher and the school system. It is preferable for the teacher not to worry about observations and to believe that supervisors can recognize the good job the teacher is doing. You can meet this challenge in a matter-of-fact way by planning for and expecting regular observations. It can be valuable to listen carefully to suggestions made for improvement.

It is helpful if the supervisor gives notice of the time of the anticipated visit, so the teacher can choose to teach a lesson that is representative of his or her skill at that time. The teacher can also prepare a short summary lesson plan to give to the supervisor before the observation. This will help assure that the observer knows the plan and goals and doesn't miss points the teacher makes.

If the teacher can develop an attitude that observers and visitors are welcome at any time in his or her classroom, it seems to lower tension about being observed. Be welcoming and flexible about these short disruptions to the teaching message. Make sure each visitor has an appropriate seat, introduce him or her to the class, and then get back on task in a matter-of-fact way.

From long experience, I believe it simplifies life to just teach every day following the lesson sequence suggested by the school system. In this book, I suggest a general plan that includes a clear statement of an objective, a warm-up, a short review of previous work and homework, an overview and explanation of why the new lesson is presented, an introductory activity, developmental activity, and closure.

If a teacher has consistently followed a logical professional plan each day, it becomes less threatening to teach the plan during a supervisor's observation. A teacher who has made a habit of organizing all daily lessons following the recommended plan is more comfortable and sharp, which should result in a positive observation.

The professional observer looks for several things. Generally he or she has a form provided by the school system directing the observation. Some of the main points considered may be planning and preparation, learning climate, instruction skill, professionalism, and achievement outcome. The observer will probably take notes and will rarely participate in the class.

Children may or may not behave well during periods when supervisors are observing their teacher. Cooperative student behavior is not a factor one can count on. Sometimes students are intimidated and are unusually quiet and docile. Other days, certain students take a peculiar pleasure in misbehaving, perhaps to gain attention from the teacher and the visiting supervisor. Happily, many times students act in their normal fashion, which can be comfortable for the teacher.

Following the observation, there should be a time for a personal conference with the supervisor. Endeavor to find a time that will not be rushed and meet in private. Try to be professional and businesslike about the comments made. Hopefully the supervisor is trained to emphasize positive aspects of the class he or she evaluates. Be careful not to react emotionally to suggestions and criticism. Try to accept the recommendations in an objective manner. Change and self-improvement are important aspects of successful teaching.

If you disagree with a point the supervisor makes, ask politely to have this suggestion clarified. Explain the intentions or reasons for what was done, if that may clear up the situation. Don't stew over criticism. Focus on the positive aspects of teaching.

Observations are intended to improve teaching and schools. Teachers learn to become familiar and comfortable with these visits. Preplanning of the lesson and self-discipline to remain objective and calm help. Welcome many visits and give a sense of openness to the classroom.

Parent Volunteers

Most teachers could really use some help in their classrooms. A day never seems long enough to get all the planning, directed teaching, paper and project corrections, housekeeping, recording, and similar jobs done. Parent volunteers, if available, can do numerous tasks to help. Several students can benefit from one-on-one help or tutoring. Fresh bulletin boards and showcases can be created. Handouts can be reproduced on copy machines. Supply items for craft projects can be cut or assembled to be ready for children. New books can be marked. Papers can be filed. Word processing can be accomplished. Banners and signs can be made on paper or on the computers. Bulletin board letters and seasonal items such as turkeys can be cut out. Photos or video pictures can be taken. Milk money or product sales money can be counted. A child may be helped to tie shoes or get a hat and coat on. Science equipment can be cleaned and stored away. Art projects can be hung on the walls. Computers can be turned on or shut off properly. Field trips and parties can be chaperoned. The list of possible teacher-help jobs for volunteers is endless.

Parent volunteers can come into the classroom on a regular basis to assist with these jobs. Some schools provide a coordinator or assign a school secretary to direct these volunteers to teachers who wish to work with them. Some teachers request volunteers in letters they send home with children or ask for them on back-to-school nights and similar occasions.

It is important to make sure volunteers are made to feel useful and are given a variety of tasks to do. A volunteer may get the feeling he or she is not needed if the teacher has not planned tasks for the volunteer. When a volunteer realizes there is no substantial contribution to be made, he or she will not come back. Sometimes being given too many boring, repetitive tasks drives volunteers away, too.

A teacher who utilizes the services of volunteers successfully gives time to the planning of tasks to be completed. It can be helpful for the teacher to begin by making a list of possible tasks for the volunteer to do. This can be kept in a volunteer folder or notebook, where both the teacher and volunteer have access to it. Information such as class schedule, names of students, names and positions of staff members, a map of the school, and certain school policies and rules could also be included in the notebook. When the volunteer arrives, the teacher may not immediately have an opportunity to explain tasks. The volunteer can then check the notebook and pick a job that can be begun on the volunteer's own initiative. As the teacher finds time during the class to direct the volunteer, he or she may change task assignments to have the volunteer complete something more pressing.

The teacher should make sure the volunteer has a secure place to stow a purse or coat. A comfortable chair should also be made available. Remember to encourage him or her to take a lunch break and insure that the volunteer can purchase lunch and eat it in an appropriate place.

Volunteers often gain great personal satisfaction from helping in a school. It can be immediately evident that the class benefits from having two adults with them. Children often behave better when the volunteer is near them. Some volunteers work one-on-one with children or with small groups, which helps the children get needed attention. The volunteer can complete housekeeping, paper correcting, or tasks such as those listed above, freeing the teacher for more directed teaching time.

Parent volunteers do need to understand that any information they gain about children is to remain confidential. They should be coached on appropriate educational methods and practices in a school system. They especially need to be careful of what they say and rules about touching children. Some school systems provide volunteer training sessions to cover these matters. The teacher should objectively discuss with the volunteer any problem that arises, not being in the least reluctant to correct it. The teacher needs to speak sensitively, of course, dealing with facts and explaining the reasons for the volunteer to change the inappropriate practice.

Volunteers are often parents, who appreciate their closer understanding of the school because of this participation. They can be a positive communication force in the community and serve as advocates for the school. Schools that work closely with parents and communities to meet student needs can be more productive.

Some volunteers appreciate tributes, certificates, special teas and luncheons, etc., to recognize their service. Others would prefer to make their contributions to the school privately. Students, teachers, and the school system can benefit from successful volunteer programs and should welcome them.

Advanced Study and Workshops

Pursuing advanced study for teachers on a regular basis is a bit like making systematic payroll investments for financial security. In-service training, seeking a higher degree, and attending workshops are like investing in oneself and in the teaching career. A teacher shapes and refines teaching skills with advanced study.

This is a technical age, so it is important for teachers, as leaders in our country, to be abreast of the times. The children being taught are aware of new developments. Teachers should be part of the same enthusiasm to be "with it" in the modern world. We live in a world of constant change. Teachers who do not resist change and are willing to step up to change and learn new ideas will thrive.

It takes precious time to attend workshops and undertake advanced study, but one simply needs to schedule this on a regular basis. Maybe it is appropriate to designate one evening a week. Some teachers attend weekend courses offered by some colleges. Other teachers devote more time than this to professional study. If one participates in study and development regularly, even in small increments, it adds up to make a changed and more professional person.

There may be an exception to scheduling professional development time for mothers or fathers with high responsibilities for their own children. These parents may need to defer attending the study classes to a time when their own children do not need them at home so much. However, it is possible to take some courses via television or the Internet at home, if that can be worked out. Teachers know their own family's needs have to come first.

Advanced study develops more than a teacher's skills and knowledge. It also can improve a person's poise and self-esteem. There are also many pleasant social contacts to be gained in adult classes. The classes can help in meeting certification requirements and professional status and titles. Often advanced credit or degree completion raises the salary of a teacher. So many teachers are underpaid that this becomes a big reason to take more classes.

In addition, advanced study provides an outlook on other fields where one might possibly wish to work. You may find new opportunities in specialties, administration, etc. A teacher also meets many professional contacts while furthering education. The combination of a wider outlook and increased connections may enhance one's teaching effectiveness, also.

Proponents of "improving education" always list improving the teachers as part of their "better schools" plans. It is necessary for teachers to recognize that they do play this important role of providing quality education for children. Teachers need to upgrade their skills and be up with the times and demands of today's society. Most teachers who organize their time to get schoolwork done at school can find time for advanced study to develop as strong and up-to-date teachers. It is important to schedule professional development as part of your teaching career.

Chapter 7

🐾 🐾

Professional Methods

Teaching Objectives

A teacher should be clear about what he or she intends to teach. Through the years school systems have varied the term for what is taught. This can be referred to as objectives, concepts, principles, or goals. The important point is that the objective is clearly understood and communicated to students.

Some teachers present material in a piecemeal fashion. They will direct students to study certain pages in a book about Native Americans or poetry or the letter *B*, for example. They do not focus on objectives such as identifying reasons and factors that led to the American Civil War, recognizing Native American contributions to American culture, understanding the creation of poetry as a form of literature, or listing words that sound a certain way because they have the letter *B* in them.

I have been frustrated observing some haphazard teacher presentations in the past. One teacher gave each child a plastic bag of glitter objects and confetti, which was supposed to teach students to consider all people as bright and different. Nothing was done to present a clear objective before this and nothing was done to develop this idea following the distribution of the bags. Another teacher gave squares of cardboard to each group of four persons in her class. Students were to stand, crowded together, on the cardboard and recognize that relationships are important. However, there was again no clear objective stated before the activity and no development of the concept after it. The experience was meaningless and a bit silly for most students. If one is going to teach about relationships, there is much more to include: empathy, communication, value, eye contact, timeliness, skills, and so on.

Institutions teach education students to follow a format like Bloom's Taxonomy. This includes using action or thinking words to describe knowledge, comprehension, application, analysis, synthesis, or evaluation. Future teachers memorize this structure with the mnemonic: "Keep calm at all sports events," which includes the first letter of each. Taxonomy-based objectives can be introduced with verbs, such as *observe, contrast, paint, classify, combine*, or *judge*.[1] It actually can be helpful to express objectives in this professional manner. It forces a teacher to be clear about what is to be taught in that lesson. With experience, a teacher can state objectives spontaneously without referring to the Bloom structure.

As a lesson is developed, each segment should be related to the teaching objective. If the lesson objective is to recognize contributions of Native Americans to American culture, the warm-up could be to alphabetize a list of twenty-five words in common American use that come from Native American languages. An overview of the lesson would be to discuss with the students why contributions of this culture have enriched the United States. Perhaps students could share firsthand knowledge of experiences with Native Americans from their own families or travels or reading. An appropriate introductory activity might be to watch a film about uses of medicines and herbs that have been taught to us by Native Americans. A developmental activity would be to research Native American games, foods, crafts, significant leaders, nature principles, and beliefs. Groups of children or individuals could be assigned specific topics to research in library books or on the Internet. Brief reports on this research would share the information learned with the whole class. Another developmental activity could be to assemble a god's eye-type cross out of popsicle sticks and yarn. (God's eyes are Southwestern Indian ceremonial shields. They were called god's eyes because through them a god might keep a watchful eye.) A closure could be asking students once again to list terms and words our nation has gained from Native Americans.

Teaching in a professional and meaningful fashion is an educator's goal. Seriously developing objectives to clearly explain what is being taught and connecting the teaching lessons to the objectives is important. Beginning lessons by stating the objective helps make efficient use of time and increases organization, understanding, and teacher clarity.

Time Management

If a new teacher wanted advice about time management, a valuable recommendation would be to attempt to complete all schoolwork in a nine-hour workday. If classes begin at 9:00 A.M., this would mean that the teacher would arrive at school by 8:00 A.M. and stay until 5:00 P.M.

The teacher would not bring bags of work home and would have each evening and weekends for his or her own life. If all teachers did this, a community would recognize that teachers put long hours into planning, teaching, housekeeping, and evaluating student work. Teachers who leave school early and do schoolwork long hours at home give the impression that teachers work short days, from 8:45 A.M. to 3:00 P.M. The community assumes these teachers have free time when the students are not there. If a teacher begins the profession with strong self-discipline to keep schoolwork at school, he or she *may* be able to continue this practice throughout a teaching career.

Time management is also an important part of class management. It is important to be ready for a class on time. Papers and materials can be laid out before the children arrive. Students can be encouraged to begin the warm-up right away. A teacher can observe when a large portion of the class has finished an assignment and move on to the next activity. Students who have not finished can be instructed to complete this work when the class moves on to a period of developmental activity, just before closure of the lesson, or at some other appropriate time.

Managing transitions from one activity to the next is important. *Transition time* is the time it takes to move from one learning activity to the next. The teacher needs to give clear instructions about collecting work, books, and supplies and explain what students are to do next. An example might be: "We are finished with our warm-up. This is what I want you to do. First, put your warm-up into the science section of your notebook. Then take out your science book. Open the science book to page 375." Behavior during transition needs to be monitored by the teacher. It is wise to allow a bit of movement, because activity is beneficial for children. Students may move to return papers, find books, locate new supplies, etc. The teacher must ensure that students are orderly and getting ready for the change.

This focusing the class on beginning a new activity is part of the emphasis of "time on task," which aids learning efficiency. Students and teachers can dawdle along and waste a good deal of time. The teacher needs to observe the class and note who is putting forth effort, moving to a child who is not working. Simply looking at the child and the book may get it open. A quick reminder, such as "The book, page 375," may do it. Some teachers open the book for the child themselves. Each management technique helps motivate the child to get to work. Again, this new activity may be changed when a large part of the class finishes it. It may be possible to move individual students to the next activity as soon as they are finished. If it is more appropriate to move the whole group on at one time, the teacher may wait until a large part of the class is ready or may decide to change at a certain time by the clock.

It is usually helpful to estimate time allowances for each lesson segment. This can be included in the lesson plan. Examples of this would be "Warm up: seven minutes; review, objective, and why: three minutes; introductory activity: fifteen minutes; developmental activity: fifteen minutes; clean-up and closure: five minutes." The teacher would need to keep an eye on a watch or a clock regularly. It may seem a bit forced and regulated to follow a time schedule, but a general time schedule helps keep the teacher moving toward accomplishment of the goal for each lesson. Of course, there are exceptions in the exciting world of teaching and learning. There will be times when discussions become exceptionally interesting and meaningful and deserve to be extended. There will be times when the whole class needs more time to complete the objective. Teachers need to be flexible and adapt to a new plan.

It is valuable to establish routines in the classroom that will enhance time management. Always show students how the material they have just learned is related to the new material. Posting daily activities on the blackboard aids students in beginning work as they note the appropriate time. Students should clear desks and have tools ready as soon as they arrive. A routine should be established for giving out and collecting materials, with some papers and materials accessible as students enter the room. Locate some special materials students may get to use when they complete work early.

At the end of a class, it is courteous for a teacher to allow students a few moments to gather their materials together, and it is essential to excuse students on time. When one plans and charts out timeliness into the lesson, one can regularly excuse students on time.

Student Thinking

Teachers hold some responsibility for encouraging and developing student thinking. There is great pressure on educators to teach children to score well on standardized tests. This is a worthwhile goal, but teachers know that, in addition, the child needs to be able to think independently for success. There needs to be a compromise between test-ready students and students who are encouraged to think creatively and solve problems.

Teachers can ask questions in a continuum of steps that develop thinking skills. Various thinking frameworks that assist students with question development are called "Think Trix," "Questions for Life," and similar titles. An example of "Questions for Life" question categories in order of thinking challenge is:

Perception or recall (lower cognitive level)
Induction
Analysis
Same/Different
Insight
Appraisal
Summary
Evaluation
Idea
Prediction
Action or create (higher cognitive level)[2]

Teachers practice developing strategies to include questions of all types for their students to challenge their thinking skills. Focusing on thinking skills helps students improve their ability to apply learned skills in areas of everyday life.

Probably more important than how teachers ask questions is the way some teachers create new experiences for students. Figuring out the area of a classroom or school playground will teach measurement better than answering problems from a book.[3] Handling and using food-measuring equipment and then preparing a blender drink, using a dry measuring cup, a liquid measuring cup, and a set of measuring spoons, links the learning to a real-life experience. It is also enjoyable for the class to share the blender drink. It is beneficial to teach naturally energetic students with activities. Teachers need to incorporate many appropriate activities to motivate children and help them enjoy learning.

Activity learning demands extra effort from the teacher. It can involve setting up field trips, accumulating special supplies, developing plans that assign responsibilities, gaining cooperation from students for cooperative on-task behavior, and patience with trial-and-error learning. Contacting people in the school and community, preparing a valid grading standard, and giving clear explanations of directions are also important.

Computers can be tools for development of high-level thinking. This is not true when they are used simply to tutor children in remedial work or programmed learning. Several software programs, such as *Oregon Trail*, develop thinking skills. *Oregon Trail* has a game format that allows children to make choices when going west in the days of the Oregon Trail. Developing a lesson using *Power Point*-type programs develops thinking skills. *Power Point* is a Microsoft program that incorporates graphics and written ideas in a page-sequence story on the computer. Including use of digital cameras and video cameras into programs is another strategy for thinking development. Research on the Internet, or in the library, can be set up to develop thinking skills.

A teacher who develops thinking skills with students gains rich satisfactions. This adds a full dimension to teaching. Students are generally motivated and interested. School is an active, vital place—more like the real world.

Why, Why, Why?

"Why do we have to learn this?" is the thought that goes through most students' minds when a teacher introduces a new concept to the class. "Why do we have to learn fractions? or adverbs? or Civil War history?" The teacher will need to confront this resistance and present the new material as being useful or of interest to the student. The teacher, who clearly understands the value of the knowledge, should explain it in a clear, convincing manner. Students who have been given this beginning mindset will be more receptive to learning the new lessons.

Teachers can explain why the new lesson material is important by referring to a film, current newspaper, magazine, or life experience, or by having the students research the topic or read about it. The conviction of the teacher in the importance of this subject is crucial in conveying the significance to students of why they should learn something. Modeling, role example, and sincerity are clearly read by students.

Another way to give the students insight into why they need to learn something is to ask them. Have them brainstorm "Why should we learn fractions? the food triangle? the difference between *their, there,* and *they're*? or how to read music?" The teacher can divide the class into groups of three or four students and give each group a large piece of lined chart paper and a large marker (or a piece of notebook paper and a pencil). Tell the student groups to each choose a leader and a recorder. Set a feasible number of expected reasons for each group to list (perhaps five for a top grade). Set a time limit for the activity.

Students should title the paper with the statement "Why We Study Fractions" (or whatever topic was chosen). The recorder should number the paper at the left margin and print the group's reasons. The recorder should also list names of group members in the lower right corner.

When the teacher feels the class is ready, the lists are collected. This is an important teaching opportunity. The teacher can hold each list up, so all can see. One student from each group is asked to read one good idea from the group list. The teacher may add comments to strengthen or clarify points, add factors of merit, and summarize important values to the new lesson concept. This student-led introduction to the value of a sensitive or difficult lesson idea makes a strong beginning.

Teach the End First

Special educators have developed a number of techniques that can apply to all students. "Teach the End First" is one that develops a teaching lesson well in a child's mind.

In working with students of limited ability, teaching the end step first, then the next to the end, and so forth, seems to work well. An example of this is teaching these students how to change a tire. The child is taught how to put the wheel cover on first and the lug nuts next. Then her or she is taught how to settle the good tire on the rim and work it on, etc. An expert patiently teaches each step in reverse order. Eventually, the child learns the whole procedure and can do the whole process from beginning to end in the right order.

This plan works successfully for regular students, too. An example is the use of the "Teach the End First" technique in a regular classroom for a research assignment. The teacher would announce the research project, discuss what its objective is, and why the class members are being assigned this project. Then, the teacher would explain how the project is to be evaluated and graded. This would be a time to show fine examples of previously completed projects, perhaps passing them around for children to see. Observing excellent completed work stimulates students to be creative, because seeing an actual project helps them to gain insights on how to do their own tasks. Looking at high quality projects inspires students to do as well or better on their own assignments, too.

The next step would be to clearly explain when the research projects are due and how to turn them in. Make sure each child writes the due date in his or her assignment book or notebook. Then state the rules for choosing subjects, format, length, etc. You would discuss where to find resources and find out what availability students have to the media center or a library or computer encyclopedia or the Internet. You would want to explain how to verify resource information. Many teachers would provide this information in a fact handout sheet. The due date can be repeated on this paper, too.

Then a topic or topics for the project would be discussed more fully. Students could brainstorm ideas to help formulate the topic. They should find it easier to choose topics by having so much information already. It is comfortable for a child to focus on an idea for a project once it is more real in his or her mind. The student will undoubtedly be thinking about his or her commitment throughout the teacher's presentation.

Students may be ready with more meaningful questions after being led step by step through the assignment by teaching the end first. High quality projects should be the result.

Teaching the end first also relates to using rubrics. Some teachers use rubrics to detail requirements for an essay. Others consider a rubric as a set of rules for an assignment. As one wrote, "It can cover every aspect of an assignment, from the length of paragraphs to the placement of topic sentences to the numbers of supporting points."[4] In some cases a rubric is a grading guide, telling students they will get an *A* or a *4* for certain criteria and lower grades for fewer points of content. An example of a grading rubric follows this section.

Some school systems and teachers believe the rubrics provide very precise standards which will clearly help students do excellent work. However, other educators think the rubrics reduce creativity. Teachers may also find the rubrics tie them to scorekeeping and limit their freedom to correct as they wish. Rubrics can also make student work slower to correct for a teacher.

Example of a Scoring Rubric

Scoring Rubric

4 = Task response is clearly developed, complete, accurate, with complete sentences for warm-up

3 = Task response is clear, fairly complete and accurate, with complete sentences for warm-up

2 = Task response is partially developed, but explanation may be muddled

1 = Task response is attempted, but may be incomplete

0 = Non-scorable response (NSR)

Developing Creativity

Students enjoy being creative. Teachers who want to encourage creativity need to build it into the lesson plan from the beginning of class, or even before class starts. The teacher needs to focus on ways the lesson can be completed imaginatively.

It may encourage student creativity to suggest alternative assignments. Perhaps students could complete the same assignment with a poem, one-page written assignment, well-done poster drawing, small booklet, rap verse of twenty lines, comic strip of ten frames, or model. This type of variety relies on the belief that students have multiple intelligences or that they have varying learning styles. Each of the suggested assignments is specific and would need to be explained, with an explanation of how it would be graded and what would be expected.

A poster could be displayed to illustrate the choice of assignments:

Alternate Assignments

1. Write a poem of twelve to twenty lines.
2. Write a one-page essay.
3. Draw a twelve-by-eighteen-inch poster in color.
4. Make a six-to-eight-page booklet about the subject. Include a cover. Staple pages together.
5. Write a rap verse of twelve to twenty lines.
6. Draw a comic strip of ten frames.
7. Build a model related to the subject with clay, paper, or wood.

Providing excellent examples of each of these assignments will encourage creativity in several ways. First, it will open students' eyes to high level of work that could be accomplished. Second, it will stimulate them to think of new, perhaps better ideas. It will also eliminate the mind block some children get that they can not think of anything to do on their own. Showing examples appeals to the students whose learning styles are visual. These students gain their ideas from seeing something, not from hearing about it.

When displaying examples, teachers may fear that some students will simply copy them. This can be avoided when the teacher explains the grading rubric or grading format. One criterion point can include "demonstrates creativity."

In addition, the examples can serve as tools for certain special education students to use. Most classes have some special-needs students, some with limited reading ability and some with low dexterity. Certain students might be permitted to trace a graphic work and others could be allowed to copy part of a written assignment. Some schools encourage enlargement of such work for students with limited eyesight to observe or to copy.

Students who have high abilities could be encouraged to suggest a different assignment, specific to their own interests, to the teacher for approval. The teacher would of course have to evaluate whether the suggestion meets the lesson plan and can be weighted equitably with the teacher's alternative assignments.

Some teachers are reluctant to allow too much creativity, because it appears to be more difficult to correct the student work. This does not have to be true, however, if the teacher has planned grading criteria carefully.

Creativity can always be encouraged by simply stating that it is appreciated for any assignment. Examples of individual, outstanding work can be shown to the class when they are returned. Students will soon learn that the teacher respects and recognizes creativity on a regular basis. A bonus for the teacher and students is that new ideas are stimulating and make the class more enjoyable.

Adapting for Special Needs

Most teachers find they have special needs students in their classes. The notice, identification, and preparation to anticipate these children varies between school systems. Ideally, the teacher would have a chance to read the children's records and discuss their needs with specialized professionals prior to the first day of class. These classes would preferably have fewer pupils to allow for adapting the curriculum to these special students. However, sometimes they just arrive, and the teacher must make on-the-spot provisions for the handicapped students. There are some general ways to adapt lessons and teaching methods for them.

When federal legislation for the handicapped was passed in 1975, there were many inequities for needy children in schools. Handicapped students were generally segregated in special schools and some were not schooled at all. The law now requires school districts to provide appropriate education and related services for students with mental, physical, and emotional disabilities in the "least restrictive environment." Regular classes began accepting handicapped students in the early years following the new law, and the early programs mainstreamed one or two special-needs children at a time into these classes. Today some classes can have as many as twelve handicapped students, making up a third of the class. Special-needs students mainstreamed into classes today have more serious needs than in previous years as well.

This discussion is not meant to cover these serious situations of large numbers of special-needs students or those with serious handicaps. It is meant rather to be a general discussion for adapting lessons to classrooms with no more than three to five handicapped students, which is more typical. These mainstreamed students can have varying handicapping conditions in the same class.

It can be beneficial to let the child tell the teacher how best to help him or her, if possible. The child has been dealing with the situation for a long time. Each child has an I.E.P. (Individual Education Program), probably filed in the guidance office. This document states modifications and accommodations which are to be implemented in all classes. Health personnel, special education advisors, administrators, guidance personnel, and other teachers may assist the teacher also. Arrange for *willing* buddy students who will help coach these children in the class. Some regular students take the initiative and find satisfaction from helping another child. Do not assign students to this task, however. A child deserves to seek his or her own education in the class and may not have an interest in or want to help another for private reasons. Students who appear to require a good deal of hands-on assistance can be seated near the teacher.

Students who are blind often have a Braille typewriter to help them take notes and do classwork. Some blind students may have services of a specialist who transcribes regular classwork into Braille. A special education teacher aide to help with interpreting the lesson may accompany others. The classroom teacher serves more as a learning leader and facilitator for these adaptations. In classes where the blind student is on his or her own, the teacher must try to verbally interpret as much material as possible for the child. Some students may use a tape recorder to reinforce the lesson at a second hearing at home. There are situations in which blind students can use voice-activated computers to complete lessons also. Blind students can complete many hands-on projects and even cooking tasks, but need a trained person to coach them, one on one, to avoid accidents. A blind student can feel oven heat and burner heat in a cooking class carefully—not touching either, of course.

Children with low vision may receive some of the same services as blind children. However, these children are often left to the total responsibility of the classroom teacher. The instructor can set certain copy machines to enlarge written assignments and some text materials. Be careful to seat this child in a well-lighted area of the classroom. The child may be able to point out the best location. Blind and low-vision children can be tested orally. The teacher needs to be particularly aware of safety needs for these students during certain activity lessons.

A child who has hearing problems should be seated with his or her better hearing ear toward the center of the classroom and the instruction area. A hearing-impaired child may carry a tape recorder to listen again to the lesson at home. This child will appreciate having lesson instructions written on paper and on the board. Some teachers learn sign language if they have numbers of hearing-impaired students. Very young hearing-impaired children need consistent, clear, simple discipline messages. They are not able to interpret tone of voice as readily as hearing students, so they often miss the emphasis of a direction. Make eye contact and speak slowly with a child who has hearing difficulties. Try to speak with them with minimal background noise.

The child who is labeled mentally deficient is sometimes referred to as mentally challenged, developmentally disabled, slow, and other terms. Teachers may attempt to find reading material on a less-demanding level for some of these students. They can also simplify or adapt certain lesson assignments. Computers are often utilized to provide appropriate work. Levels of ability vary greatly among these children, so the teacher may benefit from assistance from a special education coordinator, other teachers, guidance counselors, and parents. "Teaching the End First" and "Trace, Copy, Recall" are two other sections of this book that may benefit some of these children. They can also be given certain hands-on projects related to class readings. An example would be to make a poster of healthy foods from magazine cuttings while the rest of the class is reading and writing about nutrition.

Some children are considered LD or learning disabled. An LD child may be a TAG (Talented and Gifted) child or have any range of ability below this; *LD* means that there is a significant discrepancy between cognitive and academic performance, wherever they fall on the intelligence scale. LD students have specific learning disabilities that could include visual perception, disgraphia, or auditory processing. This type of child generally appreciates patience and respect from a teacher. Sequencing material that is presented step-by-step and allowing extra response time will aid these children. Some of the suggestions for mentally deficient students can also be used for learning disabled, when appropriate to their disability.

Mute students are not able to speak words. They may need a special education teacher aide in a regular classroom to interpret material and assist with communication and/or discipline needs. This child needs a buddy or the aide for hallway trips.

Certain students have emotional or behavioral problems. There can be varying degrees and patterns of these disabilities and each requires individual placement. Some students have diagnosed conditions that make them talk out or say inappropriate words. Others may have obsessive-compulsive problems. Attention Deficit Hyperactive Disorder may mean a child needs special seating and alert attention at times from the teacher. These students often have special instructions in their written records in the guidance office. The records may give suggestions that the teacher can follow. One child's folder, for example, said it would be helpful to mark off a boundary area on his desk with masking tape; this worked to keep his hands within that area. For some reason that restrained him so he did not more out of his seat to annoy other children, also.

Teachers need some training in dealing professionally with emotional or behavioral conditions. It is beneficial to remain calm, be patient, and deal objectively with problems. In a regular class, these students often respond to patience and the firm but warm structure of clear rules from the teacher. Restless students can be seated on the perimeter of the room where there is a bit more space on one side of the child. These children benefit from counseling about their problems. It can be helpful to develop a program of incentives for modifying the child's behavior in the class. Some emotionally disturbed students work well with contracts they have agreed to. Be sure to offer praise and positive encouragement. Put extra effort into developing rapport with these students. Behavior problems with special-needs students should be dealt with privately, in the hallway, if possible. These children should not be allowed to disrupt the whole class. A first approach is to move the angry child to a new location, preferably with a bit of space around the new seat. Don't be reluctant to ask for help with these students. If a teacher has fairly worked with the problem to the best of his or her ability, a disruptive student should be removed temporarily from the class.

The health aide may advise the teacher about certain students who have a brain shunt (which drains extra fluid in the brain) or other physical problem. Some children have a trachea tube, which can be seen. The teacher needs to seat these children carefully, so he or she can see them readily and they are not in a location to be bumped or touched by classmates. Learn how to best deal with these children's disabilities from the health aide, special education supervisor, or guidance counselors. Certain children with specialized physical problems need nursing services.

Children in wheelchairs are mainstreamed into the regular classrooms. A teacher needs to provide enough space for the child, plus a table to do work on. The table may have to be adjusted to provide clearance for the student's legs and the chair. The Special Education Department will provide a table if the child does not have a tray attached to his or her wheelchair. It is wise to seat this child near a door for easy access. Another child may volunteer to serve as a regular buddy to assist the child's movement in an emergency; you may want to instruct the class to allow this child out first. Lessons probably do not have to be modified for this child, unless they require activity. It's surprising what mobility these children acquire, even dancing in the wheelchair at a school dance. Remember to provide accessibility for wheelchairs when planning class trips.

Children who are on crutches may need space and buddy considerations similar to those for wheelchair students. Tell the student where to lay the crutches in the classroom. Allow these students to leave the classroom three minutes early to move through the hallway more easily. A buddy to carry books is also helpful.

A child with one leg and a prosthesis on the other needs teacher attention for certain activities. This child may need a buddy for safe movement during a fire drill. It would be helpful to ask the child how he or she can be seated comfortably.

A child with one arm can be helped with thoughtful assistance. A large rubber band can hold pages of a book open. Weights or tape could be provided to help hold an assignment down for precise work. A ruler could also be taped down in a math, art, or drafting class. The computer is also helpful for some assignments for this student. A wooden board with a long nail driven through it may be used to pierce certain three-dimensional projects for this child. Examples of three-dimensional projects would be clay figures in art class or a potato to peel in a foods class. The board acts as a platform and the nail points upward. Be careful with this sharp modification item.

Some children are identified as having multiple handicaps, such as being mute with one arm. Or the child might have a trachea shunt and be developmentally disabled. Many of the multiply handicapped students are developmentally disabled. Special education teacher aides generally accompany these students in regular education classes. These aides help by interpreting the regular teacher's instructions, helping the child perform work, assisting with discipline, and escorting some children in the hallway.

Grading handicapped children is a long-term discussion for teachers. Can one set different standards for them? Each teacher has to answer this in a personal way unless there is a school system policy in the matter. You need to set goals and benchmarks for all children, but these may be modified if you choose. It seems comfortable to most teachers to assign an average grade to the handicapped child, with a higher or lower grade if they clearly merit these. Some handicaps do not require different grading from the regular students.

Adapting for large numbers of handicapped students can be overwhelming, especially when a teacher has large classes. Teachers feel guilty that they can not prepare enough special worksheets or that the special-needs student is not learning as much as the other children. Rather than become too frustrated by not providing a perfect situation, remember the purpose of mainstreaming is to give the handicapped student the most normal environment possible. The student wants the socialization with regular students and is learning to adapt to the real world.

Some teachers fear the handicapped and are not sure what these children will offer to the class. I have had students with each of the special needs listed and have gained personal satisfaction from working with them and meeting the challenges they gave. Fellow students generally were affectionate and matter-of-fact about accepting handicapped students. These children are students first and disabled second. We do not fear teaching visually impaired children with regular classes. We learn to modify for other disabilities as well.

TRACE	COPY	RECALL
respect		
safe		
orderly		
work		
quiet		

Modifying Lessons for Special-Needs Students

There are some general ways to modify lessons for special-needs students. Lessons need to be modified for other handicapping conditions as well as for the developmentally disabled. For example, finding reading materials on a lower reading level may be appropriate. There are simple tests to count words for this, and some books state their reading level in the front. The teacher can circle numbers on the regular class assignment sheet to shorten it for the special-needs child, who is instructed to answer only the circled numbers. A teacher may select only a portion of the questions from a test for special students. Printing materials is usually preferable to providing them in cursive writing for children with low reading skills. Perhaps another student could read test questions to a handicapped student. Allow more time for special students to complete assignments. Hands-on projects, such as teamed science experiments, are sometimes helpful. Use visual-teaching presentations, such as showing a picture of a tornado as that spelling word is being taught.

An example of a modified vocabulary or spelling lesson is using a "Trace, Copy, Recall" sheet. You can use these sheets for

Trace, Copy, Recall Lesson Example

Date _____ Name _____

Subject/Mod. **Language Arts** _____ Title **Spelling** _____

Assignment **Rules** _____

TRACE	COPY	RECALL
1 respect		1
2 safe		2
3 orderly		3
4 work		4
5 quiet		5
6		6
7		7
8		8
9		9
10		10
11		11

3/8 Inch

Blank Trace, Copy, Recall

Date _____ Name _____

Subject/Mod. _____ Title _____

Assignment _____

TRACE	COPY	RECALL
1		1
2		2
3		3
4		4
5		5
6		6
7		7
8		8
9		9
10		10
11		11

3/8 Inch

almost any level of student or any subject. They can also be used for regular class students. Trace, Copy, Recall sheets need a basic explanation: The child traces the first word in the left column. He or she then copies that word in the center column, with the third column folded back. The child finally tries to recall and print the word in the third column. These three steps are repeated for all five words. A child who is done early can print new words or more of the same words on the spaces below the original five. A sample Trace, Copy, Recall lesson and a worksheet and a blank Trace, Copy, Recall form are shown on the pages 123 and 124.

Technology in the Classroom

Use of technology in the classroom changes every day. However, some of the old audio-visual (AV) materials, such as tape recorders, filmstrip machines, VCRs, and computers, stay in use for a long time. A teacher who keeps up with the various uses of technology can appeal to students and enhance teaching. Children of today are immersed in electronic media. Schools benefit by entering the children's world to make education more familiar and comfortable. Many students are visual and auditory learners and profit greatly from lessons directed to their needs.

It takes a short time to get familiar with each piece of AV equipment. Ease at managing the controls, connections, and adjustment of a VCR will allow the teacher to smoothly integrate videotapes into the classroom lesson. Teacher competence in this area will help prevent classes from becoming restless while a film is run backward or forward to get to the right spot or the teacher hunts for the proper connection in the back of the equipment. A teacher needs to be prepared to remedy changes in wires or cables that mischievous students may make as well.

Schools should have a person available to show teachers what is necessary in order to run all equipment. It could be a designated media specialist or another teacher who is *competent* to help. It is important to take the time necessary to master the equipment used. Each new model is slightly different.

Teachers should be able to master skills with equipment, since so many young students gain technology skills so quickly. *After* the teacher knows how to use a piece of equipment, a student can be assigned to that task. Be wary of allowing all willing students to manipulate school equipment. It is wisest to designate one or two students as being responsible to run the machines and keep them working. Arrange to have these students trained to do this, or train them yourself. Untrained and irresponsible students can accidentally break equipment at a fast pace. Then the whole lesson with audiovisuals is over.

Another general rule for use of technology is to be clear about the use of it in the lesson. Students need to know how the Internet program on whales, for example, fits into their study of oceans. They want to know why a short clip of Gaston's wooing of Belle in Walt Disney's *Beauty and the Beast* is an example of implied harassment of women and their goals. The teacher might explain how seeing a filmstrip on good table manners may help students get a job if the job interview is over lunch or dinner. Children need to know that reading a Spanish paragraph into a tape recorder and listening to it being played back, with teacher evaluation, can show them where to improve pronunciation, etc.

It is valuable, when using technology, to tie it to the project or a written report. A three-column graphic organizer, which can be adapted for many audio-visual presentations, is suggested in the next chapter. Teachers can integrate visual, auditory, or computer material into written or oral reports or hands-on projects. It is wise to establish rules about not illustrating or featuring certain negative images such as guns, beer, liquor, or inappropriate language or dress.

Using audio-visual equipment, such as a laser disc player, can make science study come alive. Images can show ocean waves in motion, experiments step by step, etc. Science students benefit from certain filmstrips and movies, too. Biology students can create a database to distinguish between terrestrial and aquatic animals, using the Internet or encyclopedia software programs and a data processing program. Computers can project views from a microscope for a whole class.

Tape recorders, often with earphones, are used in language classes to help children hear the language and record their own readings for evaluation and study. In reading classes, the more limited reader can use earphones and tapes to read a story while following the words along in a book. Some special education students record classroom lessons with tape recorders for repeated listening for reinforcement of learning. Tapes and CDs are used in chorus, band, and instrumental music classes to present musical pieces and techniques and to record music students play.

Computers can also be used to help children understand and compose music. They can run tutorials in math, science, social studies, nutrition, etc. Computers can move robotic arms in a technology program. They also help figure out design problems in technology or dressmaking. They can virtually create a home for interior design students to decorate.

Software programs can help students write stories and record them as plays for drama or English classes. The class can then videotape their own performances of the plays, with digital or regular video cameras. Skilled students can edit the video, using video software computer programs, adding or changing sound and pacing. They can also create multimedia productions from this project.

Software programs can inspire students to think and make decisions about bringing a group through a historical simulation, almost as a game in social studies. A longer social studies project would be for groups of students to create their own city or state on the computer. This project could then be transferred to a videotape or CD. These children can research in books, a software encyclopedia, and the Internet to produce their original productions. Another type of research project is called a Web Quest. These are designed to make students think creatively about "real world" problems.

Children can draw or inupt and change graphics with art software programs. They can make printed projects, computer-displayed projects, or video-displayed projects. There are special drawing tablets that can be connected to a computer to allow for more freedom of movement. Student artwork can be scanned on a scanner and inserted into a computer as a picture or as part of a book or written project. Students can print their artwork or graphics on T-shirts or fabric with special transfer papers.

Digital cameras can take pictures directly for video, be entered into a computer, and produce still pictures to print on a printer or to be used in a computer project. These, enhanced by art and graphics work, can be used in a computer-generated newsletter. Classes may use the newsletter to inform parents about what the class is doing. Other classes put their newsletter on a class Web site, so parents can access it on the Internet from home computers.

When teachers take children on field trips to museums or nature parks, the students can take pictures with a digital still or video camera. Then, when they return to the school, students can download these films on a computer, select the best photos, and write stories about what they learned. Regular camera snapshots can also be scanned with a scanner and entered into computer projects, or a regular video camera can be used with special adapters for this purpose.

Every week, there are new innovations down each of these technological paths. Every one of these projects requires a good deal of learning time or training, so it is usually necessary for a teacher to decide which path of the new technology to follow and learn. Probably no one could learn all of them. It can take an entire school day and three hours at home for the teacher to develop some of these projects. A forty-five-minute planning period simply does not afford the time needed. It also takes weeks to comfortably manage the program with students.

Schools need to help teachers with training and time to learn audio-visual skills, especially for computers. Teachers also need to develop lessons which involve scope, sequence, and evaluation for the computer projects they do. Businesses sometimes spend 60 percent of their computer money on training. Schools are behind in this aspect of needed support.

School systems have moved from using special computer labs to having four or five computers in each classroom, with computer lessons integrated with the curriculum in that class, plus more computers in the library for research. The computers available in each classroom can be used by the teachers to keep records, record grades, and develop written materials, too. Many schools are now again adding computer labs, in addition to the integrated classroom computers. The function of these new computer labs is to teach computer technology skills as a subject. In addition, educators have found that computer labs serve some purposes better, such as math remediation and full class teaching of certain concepts, allowing all members of the class to participate together. Educators believe technology improves student achievement, because it meets so many different learning styles.

Each teacher should have access to a computer in his or her classroom for keeping roll, grades, plans, lesson preparations, personal research, and professional business. Technology is an important part of the world today and is essential in classrooms.

Giving Tests

A big part of a teacher's job in testing is to make children comfortable while taking tests. Some children are nervous and tense about testing. A pleasant, congenial, relaxed climate in a classroom helps these children. A teacher should strive to establish this warm businesslike atmosphere in the room from the first day of class, for both teaching and testing. The teacher can regularly discuss test taking with the students to try to disarm their fears.

The period just before a test should not be frantic, with the teacher's giving sharp orders. This is an important time to use an encouraging, calm, matter-of-fact voice. The classroom needs to be quiet, orderly, and structured. Ensure that each child is reasonably comfortable. A child who has expressed a good deal of test anxiety can be invited to get a drink of water before the test. Make sure each child has proper supplies. Give instructions clearly and ask whether students have questions. Particularly check to see that special-needs students are accommodated for a test. Examples of such accommodations include enlarged question sheets, a simplified copy of the test, or a copy with the number of every third question circled to permit the child to answer fewer questions.

Give many tests. Give short tests often. You may also give some longer tests to challenge brighter children. It is much easier for children to get accustomed to test taking if they do it routinely. It also helps to have many test scores when giving a unit grade to a child. Many scores help you give a grade that is fair and representative of a child's total understanding.

Some teachers pride themselves on being strict and establish a cold, intimidating setting for test taking. Without resorting to this, it is essential, in a nonthreatening manner, to establish the test area so there will not be cheating. Perhaps students can spread out in the room. The teacher should stand, sit on a high stool, or walk around the room to really see what children are doing. It diminishes respect in a class if students perceive that test taking is not fair.

Before preparing a test, think about how much time it will take to grade. Teachers can get weighted down with work outside of school hours if they do not manage their paper load. Short tests are quicker to grade, and true-false and multiple-choice tests can be graded quickly with a key or a machine. Letting students correct papers can save time but can also create problems. It can be embarrassing for a student to have classmates see his or her failures, and it can also foster cheating. It is better to ask adult teaching aides or volunteers to help correct papers. Short tests may not challenge higher skilled students. True-false tests are particularly frustrating for them, because they think of other alternatives to the two basic responses and more factors than the simple question offers. Essay questions require a great deal of correcting time for the teacher, but can often encourage innovative student thinking. Decide what to look for in essay questions before correcting them. Rubrics can be valuable for valid evaluation of these written answers. It is important for the teacher to remain objective and fair in all test correcting. Grades should be entered promptly into the grade book in a clear and legible fashion.

Many teachers endeavor to test their students in a manner similar to state's special educational measurement devices. These series of tests may be called performance assessments, standards of learning, profiles of learning, etc. Another area of testing used in some school systems is for benchmarks, which are required skills and knowledge for promotion to the next grade. When teachers test in a format similar to the mandated tests, it helps students feel comfortable when they take these important tests. There is a fine line to walk when doing this, however. Teachers who heavily emphasize this similar structure of testing can be criticized for "teaching to the test."

It is important that parents and students understand a teacher's testing policy. Announce major tests well in advance. Test what has been taught. Coordinate test questions with objectives and information taught in that unit. Give children clearly legible copies of a test. Return tests and scores as soon as possible. Give make-up tests within a reasonable time. Be alert to special disabilities of students that might affect test scores. Contact parents as soon as problems are apparent.[5]

Students, parents, teachers, and the school system want to know the progress children are making, so testing is important. Testing is an important factor in allowing a teacher to know the child and to evaluate how the lessons are coming across. A teacher can reassess his or her teaching and change to work for more success. Teaching is a continuum of refining and improving how one presents ideas to students. Studying test results helps a teacher do this.

Substitute Lessons

A fortunate aspect of teaching is being able to arrange for a substitute teacher to cover classes while one must be away from school. A confident teacher can plan a substitute lesson, be assured of some student learning progress, and return to a stable classroom. However, some teachers are afraid to take time off because it causes too much disruption in their teaching program or because good substitute teachers are difficult to find.

The following suggestions assume that substitute teachers are available and able to follow an adequate substitute plan. School districts vary in standards for substitute teachers and individual substitute teachers vary in their ability to perform the job. The regular teacher needs to make a plan that will consider the qualifications expected in his or her community and tailor the plan to the expected skill level of the replacement teacher.

It is wise to leave a familiar lesson. Structure the lesson to cover the normal opening, a statement of the objective, the main assignment, developmental activities, clean-up, and closure. It is also helpful to include a general time schedule for each of these elements. List the scheduled start and stop times for each class. Clearly state which classes do which assignments. Provide a class list and seating chart for each class. Some notes can be made on the seating chart to identify a few responsible helper students.

Provide a Substitute Teacher Report Form, which can be quickly completed. It is important that substitutes maintain the attendance record, and this can be noted on this form. Allow a space for comments and for the substitute to list problems and the *names* of problem students.

The classroom teacher needs to follow-up on comments the substitute makes. Be sure to compliment classes that receive a fine report. Deal individually with each student who was a problem. This cuts down on future problems and shows respect for the substitute teacher.

Substitute Lesson Plan

Approximate Time

1 minute   **Introduce Self**

2 minutes   **Objective**

7 minutes   **Warm-up Activity**

5 minutes   **Review** (Students can be asked what they are studying or regular teacher states this on the plan)

20 minutes   **Introductory Activity** (A. Why is this lesson being taught ? B. Presenting the lesson)

5 minutes   **Developmental Activity** (More related topics to do if time allows)

5 minutes   **Closure** (Collect papers and summarize lesson)

Substitute Teacher's Form

Teacher: _____   Class Schedule: _____
Room Number: _____   _____
                                   _____
                                   _____
                                   _____

Class	Absent Students	Class Comment Students	Helpful Students	Problems

Class 1

Class 2

Class 3

Class 4

Class 5

Correct all work that was done while you were gone. Returning these corrected papers helps ensure that the students will work next time you have a substitute. It is wise to plan this assigned work with paper correcting in mind. Some teachers leave answer forms such as those for the Scantron machine which corrects papers. If the teacher leaves a reading assignment that can be answered on these forms, correcting can be done quickly. Lengthy and wordy written assignments are tedious to correct fairly.

Simplify the classroom, if you know in advance there will be a substitute teacher. It may be wise to put away scissors, crayons, and other small supplies that could be a problem. Set a tone with the class that respect and courtesy is expected from them when they have a substitute teacher. Emphasize that you will hold the students responsible for their behavior. Use needed substitute days with an assurance that the substitute will find a cooperative class.

Notes

1. Lorin W. Anderson and Karen A. Sosniak, *Bloom's Taxonomy of Educational Objectives: A Forty-Year Retrospective* (Chicago: University of Chicago Press, 1994).

2. Eleanor Kobrin and Ellen Dougherty, *Professional Refinements in Developing Effectiveness* (Nevada City, California: Performance Learning Systems, 1992).

3. Anne Westwater and Pat Wolfe, "The Brain-Compatible Curriculum," *Educational Leadership,* November 2000.

4. Jay Matthews, "Writing by the Rules," *Washington Post,* October 24, 2000, sec. A. p.13.

5. Maryland Congress of Parents and Teachers, and Maryland State Teachers Association, *A Guide to Testing for Parents, Teachers, and Students* (Baltimore, Md.: Congress of Parents and Teachers, 1994).

Chapter 8

ଚ୬୍ଦ

Learning Styles

Learning Styles

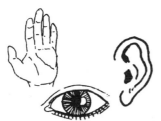 *L earning styles* simply refers to the ways people learn. Some children learn more readily from seeing an example of what is being taught, some from reading about a subject, some from hearing details from a teacher or recorded tape, and some others from hands-on projects. Not everyone learns in the same way, because not everyone's brain is stimulated in the same way.

Some educators have described variance in learning as "multiple intelligences." Howard Gardner writes "that all human beings are capable of at least seven different ways of knowing the world—ways that I have elsewhere labeled the *seven human intelligences.* According to this analysis, we are all able to know the world through language, logical-mathematical analysis, spatial representation, musical thinking, the use of the body to solve problems or to make things, an understanding of other individuals, and an understanding of ourselves."[1] Others term this concept learning channels, powers of the mind, vectors of the mind, right-brain and left-brain theory, domains of learning, etc.

137

The reason teachers need to understand learning style differences is that expanding the use of different styles in teaching presentations can make many more students understand a concept. Teachers tend to teach the way they were taught themselves or using their own personal favorite learning style. However, it can enhance teaching results and students' comfort if teachers include multiple teaching strategies in each lesson.

For example, a teacher can announce the pages of a homework assignment for students who learn easily by hearing and also write the page numbers on the board for students who understand better by seeing. Some children will concentrate by being given time to look this assignment up and focus on three important points. Teachers who are aware of varying learning styles will find that their students may be more successful with assignments.

Children usually realize that it is easier for them to learn in some classes than others. They are aware that they have learning preferences.

The results of a survey of 1,059 student assessments of their own learning styles may clarify this concept for some teachers. In this survey, seventh-grade family and consumer sciences students were requested to complete a learning styles assessment in which they were asked to read forty-five statements and decide how they felt about each. Students were given statements such as "When I do math problems in my head, I say the numbers to myself," and "I like written directions better than spoken ones." They then decided whether the statement was "most like me" and gave it four points, "somewhat like me" and gave it three points, "a little like me" and gave it two points, or "least like me" and gave it one point.

The responses were summarized into nine categories by gathering groups of related questions. The categories were Visual Language, Visual Number, Auditory Language, Auditory Number, Auditory/Visual/Kinesthetic, Individual Learner, Group Learner, Expressive-Oral, and Expressive-Written. Emphasis on Visual Language means that students learn from seeing words and remember and use information they read. Visual Number means the student works with, remembers, and understands numbers better if he or she sees them. Auditory Language means learning, understanding, and remembering words and facts best by hearing words spoken. Auditory Number means the children learn best by hearing numbers and explanations, can work problems in their heads, and may say numbers to themselves or move their lips as they read a problem. Auditory/Visual/Kinesthetic is learning by experience, doing, touching, and self-involvement. Individual Learners learn best, thinking best and remembering more, when alone. Group Learners work best with at least one other person; interaction increases their learning and recognition of facts. Expressive-Oral students can easily tell others what they know, speak fluently, and comfortably give reports or talk to teacher or classmates. Expressive-Written means children can write fluent essays and complete answers on tests and may organize thoughts better on paper than orally.

Five of the forty-five statements were assigned to each of the nine specific learning styles. The numbers the children circled for these five specific statements were summed. The totals were interpreted as: 14 to 20 equaled a major learning style, 8 to 13 equaled a minor learning style, and 0 to 7 equaled a negligible learning style. As an example, if a child listed 4,2,3,4 and 3 scores for visual statements, the total for that learning style was 16. This meant visual learning was a major learning style for that student.

The graph below is a visual presentation of the learning styles chosen by these students. It is interesting that the most prevalent learning style from the 1,059 students reported was Visual Number. The lowest choice was Expressive-Written. Perhaps this demonstration can help some teachers comprehend more about learning styles as children see them. Hopefully teachers will adapt and plan their teaching to include a wide variety of these teaching styles.

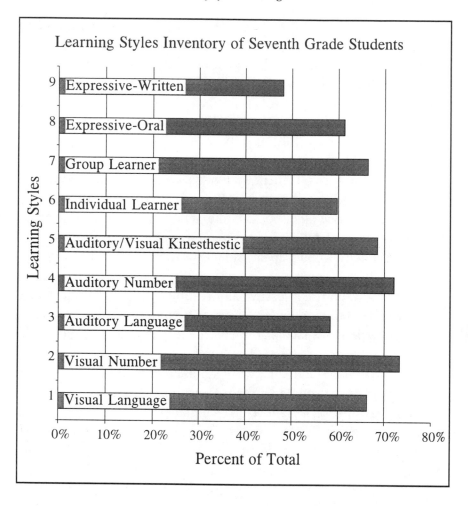

Learning Styles Inventory of Seventh Grade Students

After the children completed their learning styles assessments, the teacher and students completed two lessons to interpret and understand the learning styles. Students were then asked to report their results by carefully graphing their major learning styles on carbonized paper. These graphs were filed in their career folders in the guidance office. The second copies were made available to teachers in notebooks located in the teachers' lounge. Students carried the original copy home to explain to their families.

The class was then given a choice of developmental activities. These alternate activities were to write about their learning styles in narrative form, write a poem to include their learning styles, make small booklets, or draw an example of each (some previous examples were shown and the summary sheet had illustrations). Some nonwriting mainstreamed students made Play-Dough models of learning styles. Animated informal discussion of learning styles took place while students shared their ideas, completing this project.

This assessment and the lessons to explain it were part of the Prince George's County, Maryland, family and consumer sciences curriculum between May 1993 and April 1998. The results help to demonstrate variance in choices by children. This report does not judge validity of the assessment instrument. However, at no time during years of repeating this activity did children disagree with their results. The students seemed interested and positive about the assessments.

One copy of each assessment was sent home to parents, one copy filed in the child's guidance office career folder, and the third copy was available to teachers.

Visual Learning

 Teachers who include an emphasis on visual teaching aid many students today. Our children have grown up in a world of pictures and signs through TV, movies, computers, magazines, newspapers, billboards, and the sides of buildings and buses. Many even wear pictures and words on their clothes and shoes. More than 60 percent of the students who completed the learning styles inventory of seventh-grade students described in the previous section scored as visual learners.

A teacher who wants to tap into this learning style will list assignments and important points on a blackboard or overhead projector. Some pass out lists of assignments, grading criteria, and report outlines; use flashcards; place the letters of the alphabet on the wall; use many graphs, picture examples, and graphic organizers.

Teachers emphasize the visual by using the posters and bulletin boards in their classrooms to illustrate important lesson ideas or character ideals. These should be chosen to display boys and girls, all ethnic groups, the handicapped, and various ages of persons. Many posters use bright, inviting colors. Housekeeping, to keep wall-mounted materials neat and up to date, is important.

There are many materials available to attach posters and signs to classroom walls. A putty substance for this purpose can be used over and over again. Cork strips can be applied to walls and used to hang posters or student work with thumbtacks. A teacher needs to be aware of local school rules before fastening the cork strips or some of the almost-permanent tape materials available. Doubled-over masking tape does not hold for long, while Scotch tape can be damaging.

Visual materials can also be hung from ceilings. Special clips that fit into ceiling dividers are available for this purpose. A string line can be hung across a ceiling to attach illustrations and student work. It would be unwise to hang items from light fixtures, however.

Magnets will hold illustrative papers and signs on many blackboards. Otherwise a cord can be stretched from the left molding to the right molding of the blackboard and papers attached to this cord with clothespins. Beware of attaching items to blackboard with substances that leave sticky residue, such as tape.

An easel is helpful for visual teaching. You can attach pages of information to the top of a large one and turn them over day by day, keeping the older ones to use again or to use for reference. Small easels can be located on cupboard, bookcase, or table tops and used for displaying books, signs, or pictures.

Visual teaching techniques include holding up pictures to illustrate a point. Flannel boards have been used for decades to show changing stories. Models of things can give students learning images. Observation of experiments or procedures helps children learn visually.

Movies and videos are very powerful teaching tools. A teacher may have to check an approved school system list or procedure to use these, however. Movies and videos need to be used with structure, so that students watch them for learning concepts, not simply for entertainment or filling time. Students can be provided with study questions to answer, or can be instructed to write their own questions and answers while watching the film. A three-category graphic organizer study sheet (see the next section) is successful for many film-based lessons.

Students can also make their own video films. They can tape student actors in social studies, history, or drama classes. Family and consumer science students, for example, can illustrate successful techniques for disciplining children. Science students can photograph experiments or nature. Technology students can illustrate demonstrations or techniques. Business students can videotape successful and unsuccessful job interviews. Dance and music classes can photograph performances for replay and study. School news programs, replays of the spelling bee, and highlights of sports or science fairs appeal to visual learning. The list of ideas for videos is unlimited.

Computers open an exciting and wide door for visual learning. Students can see pictures about the subject they are studying from encyclopedias, software programs, or the Internet. Learning math can often be enhanced with games or real-life visuals on a computer. Computer art programs teach color principles and skills. Writing becomes visually different on a computer from writing on paper. There are other programs to aid social studies, music, technology, nutrition, reading, and most subject matter.

There are special programs, such as HyperStudio,[2] which incorporate many visuals into group student projects. One project could be for a student group to create a country. They could make a flag, create various maps, choose a flower, describe a government, etc. and make these into page-by-page cards (which are like frames of a filmstrip) with visuals and sound to produce a sort of book on the computer. This could then be transferred to a video.

Dress can also play a role in visual teaching. Some teachers dress in period costumes to bring alive a part of history. Students may sometimes be asked to dress in costumes to portray learning concepts. Some teachers, such as dance, business, or physical education instructors, dress to express their subject visually. Imaginative teachers find endless ways to illustrate lesson concepts for visual learning.

Plus +	Minus -	Interesting

Plus +, Minus –, Interesting

"Plus +, Minus –, Interesting" is a commonly used type of graphic organizer. It lends itself to many applications in teaching. One way to use this organizer is to structure a student activity with it. An example of this organizer's use when showing movies or videos follows below.

Students are told the name and purpose for viewing the film they are to watch. The teacher gives background information relating the film to the curriculum. It is useful to write the name of the film on the blackboard. This information could also be provided on an overhead projector or in some other manner. Names or terms that are difficult to spell can be listed and defined, too.

A graphic organizer sheet (see next page) is given to every child. Students are told to write their name, the date, and the name of the film on it. Then the teacher explains that they should each write ten sentences about the film they will see. If their sentences are positive, they should be listed in the column under Plus +. If sentences are negative, they go under Minus –. If the sentence is simply a fact or interesting, it goes under Interesting.

The teacher can post a point card or list grading criteria on the blackboard. Perhaps nine to ten sentences is an A, eight is a B, seven is a C, and six is a D grade. It is useful to offer an A+ for more than ten sentences because certain students enjoy writing or working beyond the limits. Students will want to understand that their whole total of sentences count. An A grade could be three positive, three negative, and four interesting sentences, or five positive and five interesting sentences, or ten sentences all in one column.

Graphic Organizer

Plus +	Minus –	Interesting

Students write their sentences while watching the film. There needs to be low light available so they can see to write. When the film is finished, it is beneficial to give students time to complete their assignments with the full lights on.

A teacher, to emphasize important concepts, may choose to read aloud sentences from the student papers for a summary. Children can also be asked to read from their papers when the film is finished.

This report is fairly easy for a teacher to correct and grade, because counting sentences is fast. It is also possible to gain a sense of what students focused on and understood in the film from their answers. Teachers can choose whether to correct spelling and sentence structure.

Auditory Learning

Listening is a learning style to develop for success. People often complain that children don't listen. Some teachers create special lessons to teach listening skills because they feel that many children do not listen to lessons and assignments with the comprehension they expect.

However, children of today naturally listen a great deal. You can see numerous children, almost anyplace, with earphones on, listening to their favorite music. Many live in homes where the radio or TV is always on. There is music in stores and shopping malls. Some school bus drivers promise well-behaved children they can listen to music the bus driver provides. Parents play radios, tapes, or CDs in the car.

Some teachers then demand silence in the classroom from these same children. Quiet classrooms can be useful for some learning and are often popular with some administrators. However, a gentle buzz of learning from groups of children sharing ideas is valuable, too. Understanding teachers perceive the appropriate times for quiet and for controlled conversation. The teacher knows how to tap into varieties of auditory learning.

Listening centers, with tapes and records to enhance basic skills or teach points of music or enrichment of a history lesson, can be set up to reach the auditory learning mode. Listening to tapes is an important part of most foreign language classes. Some teachers make tapes for students to listen to for missed work assignments. Special-needs students may request to tape lessons so they may listen again to the concepts at home. Children can be encouraged to make their own tapes to listen to. A teacher needs to supervise the content of tapes, of course, particularly if students bring tapes from home or make tapes to share with others. It might be necessary to have a rule that these must be played without earphones, so the teacher can listen, when needed, to avoid inappropriate language or learning content.

Auditory learners like to talk things over, and they do well in areas in which participants contribute verbally, whether in small or large groups. Teachers can develop cooperative learning lessons to allow small groups to learn from each other.

Teachers can also lead discussions with the whole group, drawing out points of value from various students. This can be particularly valuable to highlight important points following a reading assignment. Students often find this interesting and consider learning from their fellow students to be credible information they want to listen to. Teachers should be careful to call on both boys and girls and on children of varying cultures. Leading a successful group discussion takes concentration and practice. A teacher needs to allow "wait time" for certain students to compose their answers. The teacher should try not to repeat answers, if they are clear enough, because children should be encouraged to listen to what fellow students say. It shows an element of respect and develops listening skills. The discussion should be kept positive and to the point of the learning concept. Encouragement and positive feedback from the teacher for useful answers and comments are essential for effective discussion. Oral discourse may be more beneficial for some minority students. Some of them can express themselves better orally than by writing.

Teachers can enhance auditory learning by taking basic language classes in a language, such as Spanish, that is familiar to that spoken at home by a large number of students. This can help these children relate to the teacher and the group and can facilitate the students' communication and understanding.

Children who learn well with their ears often remember facts best when the facts are presented in a poem, song, or rhyming melody. This is one of the earliest methods of teaching preschool children. Most of us know the alphabet song, nursery rhymes, clock facts, etc., from these early days. Science teachers teach biology names, the order of the planets, etc., with verses. English teachers teach some grammar rules this way. Most of us still need to sing the names of the notes of the music scale.

Some teachers use music as a key to discipline. A preschool teacher will play a few bars of music on a piano or from a record and children know it is time to gather in a circle for an activity. Other songs mean other actions from the group. Some art teachers play music to aid student creativity.

Current reading instruction is giving a renewed emphasis on phonics. This teaching of sounding out letters, groups of letters, syllables, words, and sentences appeals to the listening learner. Educators who understand the responses of children to varying learning styles can appreciate why many reading teachers today use a combination of methods for teaching reading. Word recognition would be a visual method, for example.

Music is considered an important part of curriculum in most schools. Research has shown that music is related to mathematics and other areas of learning. Many students consider music their favorite area of study. Music is obviously an integral part of dance and certain drama classes also.

Lesson strategies that purposely include auditory elements will appeal to large numbers of children. The earliest learning was often oral history. Even though we are sophisticated today, we should not omit this important method of teaching students.

Hands-On Learning

A large number of students enjoy hands-on or kinesthetic learning. They like the experiencing, doing, and self-involvement. They want to handle, touch, and work with what they are learning. Children like to color, paint, cut, glue, mold, shape, manipulate computers, saw wood, pound nails, measure, pile blocks, move small pieces, make puzzles, do science experiments, build models, and sew. The list of activities is endless.

An imaginative teacher can include a hands-on project into most lessons. Students studying a story in literature, for example, can make a map showing events in the story or design clothes for the characters. Math students can manipulate pennies or small blocks to reinforce concepts. History students can act out the signing of the Declaration of Independence. Geography students can measure distances between important cities. Some teachers teach spelling words using sandpaper cut-outs of the words, shaving cream, clay, or rice to form letters and words with high stimulation to the child— or ask students to cut and paste new story words from magazines or newspaper. Science students can add two chemicals together and see a color change, rather than simply reading about it.

Some teachers give up on this vital area of teaching because children throw the pennies, talk too much preparing their drama, break the measuring equipment, lose some crayons, or simply play with the materials. It takes preparation and discipline structure to avoid these problems.

The teacher needs to make the class aware of the purpose of the activity. It is necessary that students know this is not simply play, but how the activity will teach them a concept. This need to know, along with the teacher's confident expectation of appropriate behavior, should prevent most throwing and other misbehavior. It may be important to tie a grade to completion and quality of the project, taking care to explain the grading criteria at the beginning.

To prevent the loss of supplies, the teacher can diligently organize and set up markers, crayons, or glue into numbered boxes or baskets. The number of items in each box should be consistent, perhaps ten. These would be passed out one per row or table group to assign responsibility. Groups should *not* share supplies with each other because this confuses the issue of who lost something. The teacher needs to allow enough time to pass out the supplies and to give rationale and rules for their use before the activity. The teacher needs to also allow enough time for clean-up and responsible accountability at the end of a lesson.

It helps to have a classroom with some flexibility for varying arrangements of furniture. It would be beneficial to have some space for movement, too. Desks can be lined up in squares of four desks, or students can sit in table groups. The center or front of the room may be set for open space. Beyond the open space might be a chalkboard that usually stays a bit dusty from much student use. Shelves and counter space would be organized by activities: art supplies, books, models, and student-made materials. Certain supplies are appropriately locked in cupboards or closets; which supplies varies by the teacher's experience with the classroom needs. Around the room may be many examples of student-made art pieces, macrame, and models. Science labs can have some equipment visible. The bulletin boards can contain geometric designs or maps made by children. Open space in the room can be used to act out a scene, with activities occurring frequently. The teacher can provide guidance for fine motor tasks, moving about the room or allowing students to move to the teaching area.

Students making projects are learning more than, say, how to construct a world globe. They are learning to read, organize their work, follow directions, complete mathematical calculations, conserve building materials, and accept responsibility to finish what they start. Students get excited creating a product. Hands-on learning is more closely related to life in the real world than symbolic learning. Some educators give symbolic learning, such as algebra, more respect, but by including hands-on learning, the teacher allows for individual differences in children. A combination of learning styles pleases students and can become an integral part of good education.

 # Example of a Lesson Using a Variety of Learning Styles

Objective

The objective of this lesson is for the student to identify how various learning styles affect school learning and choice of careers.

Warm-Up

Students read a page, copied from the encyclopedia or the Internet, about peanuts. During this time, the teacher can take roll, visit with a couple students to answer needs, etc. As students finish reading, the teacher collects homework, discusses homework or reviews the previous lesson. The teacher assigns the homework for the next day verbally and writes this assignment on the blackboard, then he or she asks for questions about the assignment.

Introductory

The teacher asks if anyone can define learning styles. He or she writes a good summary definition from these answers on the board or on a large chart sheet (*learning styles* means the way persons learn). The teacher then asks why students would study learning styles today. Valuable student answers are written on a large chart sheet. Students are referred to a list of reasons on the overhead projector for more reasons to study learning styles. Some of these reasons include: helps the child understand strengths and weaknesses, focus harder on trying in weak areas, can give child a reason to ask for more help with some areas of study, aids child in selecting school and college courses, helps chose a successful area for a job or career.

Next, the teacher asks students to report on what they read about the peanut. Students from all sections of the classroom, girls and boys, and students of diverse ethnic background should be called on. Interesting points to bring out include the importance of peanuts as an American crop and the various products produced from them, many from the work of George Washington Carver. It may be informative to draw a simple drawing of a peanut on the blackboard to show the structures growing from the stem that go underground to produce peanuts. Peanuts are considered protein foods in the meat group in nutrition and are the fruit of the peanut plant.

After enough information has been shared, the teacher places a construction paper model of an eye on the blackboard, with tape or a magnet, explaining that reading is a *visual* way to learn. Write the word *visual* next to the eye. Students can describe other types of knowledge they gain from watching and seeing with their eyes.

It is also true that, if some students learned from hearing students and the teacher report facts, they learned the *auditory* way. Place a construction paper graphic of an ear on the blackboard. Discuss other ways people learn from hearing information and sounds.

The teacher next puts a paper cup on a desk in the center of each group of students. This cup is for peanut shells, to keep the desks and floor clean. Two peanuts are passed out to each child. Note: use of peanuts can be dangerous to a small number of children with severe allergies to peanuts. Do not use real peanuts if this is true for any student in a class. Students with mild peanut allergies can be instructed simply not to eat the peanuts.

Pupils are asked to look at their peanuts and tell what they see. Their answers will probably include color, shape, rough surface, size, pattern in shell, etc. The teacher reinforces the fact that this is *visual* learning.

Then students are told to shake the peanuts. Some will hear the peanuts rattling in the shell. This, along with what they learn from hearing other children's answers, is *auditory* learning.

Next, students are told to break open the peanuts and eat them, if they wish to (except those with allergies), putting shells into the paper cups provided at nearby tables. The teacher invites students to tell what they learned when they broke the peanuts open and ate them. The rough feeling of the shell, the taste of the peanut and salt, and the sensation of swallowing with tongue and throat are all examples of *kinesthetic* learning. Children may want to lick their fingers a bit to taste the salt or feel the powdery sensation of it on their fingers. The class takes time to clean up the area at this point in the lesson.

The teacher explains that hands-on activities usually involve all three of the above learning styles. Other learning styles include group learning, individual learning, logical analysis, musical thinking, use of body to solve problems, etc.

Activity

This is the time when the main lesson activity is presented. The teacher may provide each student a type of learning styles assessment to complete and discuss. Another possibility would be to ask each student to take out paper and pencil and list ways they think they learn best. They could also list ways they could work harder to develop their learning styles. They could list examples of learning they have learned with each method on their lists.

The teacher might want to offer an assignment to draw an eye, ear, hand, group of students, and a student alone. These could be labeled visual, auditory, kinesthetic, group learning, and individual learning, respectively. Construction paper projects, preparing small booklets, or molding eyes, ears, and mouths from clay or Play-Dough could be other activities offered to children to reinforce the teaching concepts.

Each assignment chosen for presentation to students is explained to inform them of how this teaches them about the objective. Grading criteria are also presented before beginning projects.

Developmental Activity

Students who complete early can be encouraged to explore ideas of careers they could enter and jobs they could do, with their individual learning styles in mind. This would involve research, perhaps on the Internet or from the career materials available in the library or in the classroom. Another activity would be to write a letter to their parents or guardians to explain their learning styles to them. The teacher may provide some handouts to help the students define terms.

Closure

The class needs to be warned when the lesson project time is nearly over. A few minutes later, clean-up time is announced. After the area is in order, assigned work is collected for assessment. The teacher can lead a discussion about the variety of ways to learn and how understanding this can aid the student's scholastic and life development. One way children can use the information presented on learning styles is for students who are visual learners to ask teachers to always write assignments on the board. Pupils who are visual or hands-on persons may need to write down assignments, to take notes, and to write lists. A student may need to ask to sit nearer the teacher if it is believed that listening learning is difficult for that child. Students who like to write can choose future school classes or careers that involve writing. Students can be encouraged to discuss learning styles with their parents and to share examples and ideas they have in the future with the class.

Cooperative Learning

Cooperative learning for children is similar to real work group situations in later life. Jobs require employees to relate successfully to fellow workers. When I surveyed learning style choices for six years with seventh graders, more than 65 percent included "group learning." Other research since the 1800s indicates that cooperative learning leads to higher achievement for all students.[3] Naturally active children benefit from interactive group tasks. Understanding other individuals is one of the seven ways of knowing the world described in the concept of multiple intelligences by Howard Gardner.[4]

Cooperative learning can benefit some slower and some culturally disadvantaged students, while giving others opportunity for leadership and providing skills in social interaction for all. Vocational classes, such as family and consumer science and technology, have always used cooperative learning groups.

There are students who prefer individual study. Many teachers also dislike grouping because the activity requires structuring and stronger classroom respect and control. Some critics argue that certain children work harder while others slide along in group work. Similarly, certain parents believe their child is not graded fairly in group projects. However, the benefits of cooperative learning are strong, and it deserves a place in regular lesson planning.

Exceptional projects can be developed using cooperative learning: Student groups produce videos of an imaginary country, using a computer software program. Others write and produce plays or stage real productions. They organize dance performances. Science students develop an original machine or product. Math students form mock financial groups and graph their investment success in the stock market. Kindergarten children paint sections of a large dinosaur mural. A technology class constructs model houses. A family and consumer sciences class puts together a six-salad luncheon, one salad from each cooking group. A fourth-grade class produces a book, with each cooperative group creating one page. Project choices are limitless and can be exciting for the class and the teacher.

Cooperative learning requires detailed plans at the beginning. Teachers learn to simplify them and adapt plans to new ideas with experience. As students become familiar with the teacher's expected cooperative learning format, the process becomes easier. The original plans can be reused.

As with any lesson, a cooperative learning plan needs an objective, with the "Why do it?" clearly stated. Groups can be divided with two, three, four, or five children in a group. Divide the class into groups by the number of jobs. If there are four jobs, there should be four groups. The teacher should try to divide children so that each group is heterogeneous in terms of ability, sex, and ethnicity.

Instructions should be read and posted on a large card, displayed on the overhead projector, or given to each team on paper. A student facilitator or group leader helps members choose jobs. Teachers can create job titles to suit the project. Titles can include: facilitator, recorder, timekeeper, reporter, artist, designer, writer, graphic artist, and materials manager.

Supplies needed are divided and put into *one* box or basket for each group. A set of job descriptions or job tickets may be included in the basket. Other supplies might include a set of markers, a ruler, *one* piece of unlined paper, and *one* piece of notebook paper.

The teacher tells the group that cooperative learning success, including the interaction and contribution of each student, will be evaluated while work is being completed, as well as the product. The teacher moves from group to group, noting some comments made and team progress on a clipboard. The teacher attempts to stay in the background, offering help only when necessary.

Some time goals may be written on the blackboard as progress is being made to aid the timekeepers. When time is called, it could speed up finishing and the return of materials if tiny cups of snack crackers are offered to each member of the groups as they finish. This snack break also allows the teacher time to organize the turned-in materials to be ready for a teacher report.

The teacher first discusses the success of group work and interpersonal skills used in each group with the class. Recorders' notes and clipboard comments are of help for this teacher report. The class can help grade some projects by voting with three fingers for a good project, four for very good, and five for outstanding. The teacher will give two grades to each group, one for interpersonal skills and one for quality of work. Each child in the group receives these grades. Recorders' sheets are of help for names when grading.

A basic summary of points to include in a cooperative learning lesson plan follows:

1. Specify size of groups
2. Name members of groups or teams
3. State purpose, materials, steps
4. Teach procedures
5. Specify and teach the cooperative skills needed or choose one skill to feature (examples are "to attend or listen" and "getting started quickly")
6. Hold individuals accountable for the team's work
7. Evaluate

Cooperative Learning Job Tickets for Older Students

A critical element of successful group learning is assigning a task to each person. It simplifies organization to have sets of "job tickets" to give to each group. The students can each draw one ticket out of a hat. An example of job assignments for older students is shown below.

FACILITATOR	RECORDER
Organizes group. Helps each member choose jobs. Makes certain that everyone contributes and keeps the group on task.	Lists names of group members and jobs chosen. Keeps notes on positive thoughts expressed. Writes final summary.
REPORTER	**MATERIALS MANAGER**
Listens carefully to each team member. Encourages recorder to prepare good notes. Interprets recorder's notes and reports summary to class.	Gets and distributes materials. Collects and turns in materials when time is called.
TIME KEEPER	**WRITER, ARTIST, OR DESIGNER**
Divides total time into units for each task. Keeps group moving toward being completed on time.	Writes up, draws, or designs the project. Listens to ideas from all team members to formulate the final project.

Cooperative Learning Job Tickets for Younger Students

It simplifies organization of a cooperative learning activity to have sets of job tickets to give to each group, regardless of age or grade level. An example of job assignments for younger students is shown below.

GROUP LEADER	**MATERIALS MANAGER**
REPORTER	**RECORDER**
TIME KEEPER	**ARTIST**

Cooperative Learning Lesson
Example Manners Book

This section describes a lesson that provides a hands-on opportunity for students to participate in a cooperative learning experience. This lesson could be adapted to use for most grade levels or most subject level classes. Each cooperative team produces one page of a picture book for the class. There will be four to six pages completed. The possible subjects are limitless but could include dimensional shapes for math, manners rules for fourth grade, Civil War battles for history, orchestra instruments for music, steps in the scientific method for sixth grade, farm animals for kindergarten, etc.

The following lesson plan example is to make a book of school manners for fourth grade. This lesson could be divided into two-day segments, if it is too long for the class's attention span.

Objective

The teacher introduces the lesson to be taught by stating, "The class is going to create one picture book to make school manners more clear for everyone."

Warm-up Activity

Students are asked to list on a piece of notebook paper five important rules for school manners. An example is to stand in lines *single file*.

While the children are working on their lists, the teacher can take roll and answer a few questions from individuals. (When the lists are finished, this could be a useful time to review previous classwork and assign the new homework, so students can note it in agenda books or notebooks, if this has not been done earlier in the day or period.)

Why

Teacher now asks the class why having everyone understand the importance of school manners is essential for order and harmony in this class.

Presenting the Lesson

Next, pupils in various areas of the classroom are asked to read one important rule from their lists, without repeating the same rule another student has already given. The teacher writes some of the rules suggested on the board, a large sheet of paper, or an overhead projector. The teacher may add rules students omitted and emphasize important ones. Teachers and students can choose four to six or more rules, depending upon the number of cooperative learning groups selected for this class. These choices will be the topics for each page of the book. Students are reminded that they are going to make one book for the class on school manners. They will be divided into groups to create the pages. One rule topic is needed for each cooperative learning group. The cover can be made by the teacher on a computer or by a selected student.

Supervised Activity

The teacher divides the class into groups of four to six students. The teacher should try to divide the students so that each group is heterogeneous in terms of ability, sex, and ethnicity. Each group is given a basket that contains the following:

1. job tickets for each member (see the preceding two sections)
2. one sheet of white paper
3. one sheet of notebook paper
4. a set of ten colored markers
5. a small ruler
6. one rules topic (each basket has a different one)

The teacher gives the following directions: "Sit with your new team group. Your group will be drawing a picture, putting a title on it, and coloring the page you complete. The picture will illustrate one important school manners rule.

"You will each choose a job ticket from the basket (some small groups will need some students to choose two tickets). The facilitator organizes your group, makes certain that everyone contributes, and keeps the group on task. The recorder lists the names of the group members and the jobs they've chosen on the piece of notebook paper. The recorder also keeps notes on the positive thoughts expressed by team members and writes a final summary for your group. The timekeeper divides the total time allowed into units for each task, keeping your group moving toward being completed on time. The artist listens carefully to each team member to formulate the picture, then makes a draft picture in pencil, keeping the picture simple to stay within time limit. The graphic illustrator listens carefully to each team member and titles the drawing with clear-to-read print or decorative lettering. The materials manager colors the picture. This team member picks up and turns in the recorder's notes, drawing, basket with ruler, markers, job ticket role cards, and title card.

"Sit closely together as you work. It's OK to move your chairs and for some group members to stand behind, so all can see and work together. I am going to monitor your group work and cooperation, sharing ideas, and staying on task, and I will grade your finished product or picture page. This is the team you will be working with, so it is important to build a strong successful team. Each team member will have a role in producing this picture page. Get started quickly. You will have twenty-five minutes to complete your page."

The teacher walks around the room, perhaps with a clipboard to note points of group cooperation. A notation of the time left, with a suggestion of which step the group should be working on, should be written by the teacher on the blackboard periodically.

When time is called, it could be useful to have a tray of tiny paper cups of snack crackers to give to each group as the correct materials are turned in. This speeds up this process and gives the teacher enough time to organize the basket and two pages from each group.

Closure, Summary, Evaluation

Then it is time to debrief the group. The teacher should start first with a short discussion of interpersonal skills, such as how the group got started quickly, what strengths different groups showed in cooperative work, and ways to improve the group's work. Next, the teacher can ask the class members to evaluate each page by holding up three fingers for a good page and four fingers for an outstanding page. If possible, a quick grade for cooperation and picture quality is noted on the clipboard at this time. At the end of the evaluation, the teacher puts the pages together quickly and shows the class how it looks as a book. It can be fastened to the cover and displayed again at the next class session. At the close of this lesson, the teacher can ask the class to applaud themselves for completing a book on manners.

Cooperative Learning Job Tickets for School Manners Rules Lesson

A critical element of successful group learning is assigning a task to each person. It simplifies organization to have sets of job tickets to give to each group. An example of job assignments for the School Manners Rules Lesson is shown below.

FACILITATOR	RECORDER
Organizes group. Helps each member choose jobs. Makes certain that everyone contributes and keeps the group on task.	Lists names of group members and jobs chosen. Keeps notes on positive thoughts expressed. Writes final summary.
TIME KEEPER	**ARTIST**
Divides total time into units for each task. Keeps group moving toward being completed on time.	Listens carefully to each team member to formulate the picture. Makes draft picture in pencil. Keeps the picture simple to stay within time limit.
GRAPHIC ILLUSTRATOR	**MATERIALS MANAGER**
Listens carefully to each team member. Titles drawing with clear, easy-to-read print.	Colors picture. Picks up and turns in recorder's notes, drawing, basket with ruler, markers, role cards, and title card.

Notes

1. Howard Gardner, *The Unschooled Mind* (New York: Harper-Collins, 1991), p. 12.

2. *HyperStudio News and Information* (El Cajon, Calif.: Roger Wagner Publishing, 1997).

3. Harry K. Wong and Rosemary Tripi Wong, *The First Days of School* (Sunnyvale, Calif.:Wong Publications, 1991), p. 243.

4. Gardner, *The Unschooled Mind,* p. 12.

Bibliography

శు౧ౡ

Anderson, Lorin W., and Sosniak, Karen A. *Bloom's Taxonomy of Educational Objectives: A Forty-Year Retrospective*. Chicago: University of Chicago Press, 1994.

Bosch, Karen A., and Kersey, Katherine C. *The First-Year Teacher*. Washington, D.C.: National Education Association, 1997.

Davidman, Leonard, and Davidman, Patricia T. *Teaching with a Multicultural Perspective*. New York: Longman, 1997.

DeBruyn, Robert L. "Getting in Shape for Parent Contact." *Master Teacher* 22 (1990).

Faber, Adele, and Mazlish, Elaine. *How to Talk So Kids Can Learn*. New York: Simon & Schuster, 1996.

Gardner, Howard. *Frames of Mind: The Theory of Multiple Intelligences*. New York: Basic Books, 1993.

Gardner, Howard. *The Unschooled Mind*. New York: HarperCollins, 1991.

Ginott, Haim. *Teacher and Child*. New York: Avon Books, 1975.

Harrell, Rick. *Integrating Technology into Schools*. Alexandria, Va: Association for Supervision and Curriculum Development, 1998 (cassette tape).

Hassenslab, Joe J., and Flaherty, Geraldine. *Teaching through Learning Channels*. Nevada City, Calif.: Performance Learning Systems, 1982.

Hopkins, Ronnie. *Educating Black Males*. Albany: State University of New York Press, 1997.

Kelly, Dennis. "Separating Classes to Create Equality." *USA Today*, February 20, 1991: p. 8D.

Kobrin, Eleanor, and Dougherty, Ellen. *Professional Refinements in Developing Effectiveness*. Nevada City, Calif.: Performance Learning Systems, 1992.

Maryland Congress of Parents and Teachers, and Maryland State Teachers Association. *A Guide to Testing for Parents, Teachers, and Students*. Baltimore: Congress of Parents and Teachers, 1992.

Matthews, Jay. "Writing by the Rules: No Easy Task." *Washington Post*, October 24, 2000, p. A13.

Moorman, Chick. *Achieving Student Outcomes through Cooperative Learning*. Nevada City, Calif.: Performance Learning Systems, 1994.

Nagel, Greta K. "Looking for Multicultural Education: What Could Be Done and Why It Isn't." *Education* 119 (Winter 1998), pp. 253-62.

Robbins, Anthony. *Giant Steps*. New York: Simon & Schuster, 1994.

United States Department of Education. *Fulfilling the Promise of Technologies for Teaching and Learning*. Washington, D.C.: United States Department of Education, 1998 (pre-publication).

United States Department of Education. *What Works: Research about Teaching and Learning*. Washington, D.C.: United States Department of Education, 1986.

Westwater, Anne, and Wolfe, Pat. "The Brain Compatible Curriculum." *Educational Leadership* (November 2000). Alexandria, Va.: Association for Supervision and Curriculum Development, 2000.

Wong, Harry K., and Wong, Rosemary Tripi. *The First Days of School,* Sunnyvale, Calif.: Harry K. Wong Publications, 1991.

Index

∞∞

About the Author

℘℃℟

arol Gildner taught school for thirty years and never lost her enjoyment of working with children. She lived in six states and three foreign countries, gaining a wide understanding of people. She graduated first in her home economics class at the University of Minnesota and has a master's degree in special education from the George Washington University. She has taught education, English, literature, social studies, general science, art, home economics or family and consumer sciences, and life skills and has been a media specialist.

She has been recognized as Outstanding Teacher of Bowie, Maryland, Outstanding Prince George's County Home Economics Teacher, and the Christa McAuliffe Outstanding Teacher of Prince George's County, Maryland. She had leadership roles as head teacher for the Omaha Women's Job Corps and as creative arts team leader in Maryland.

Ms. Gildner has published articles in professional journals and a book on working with mainstreamed children. She has taught numerous teaching workshops and adult classes. For many years, she worked with student teachers, who reported that many ideas contained in this book were helpful in their classrooms. Hundreds of former students have told her how much they enjoyed and learned in her classes.